SECRETS

OF A SOUL

PADRE PIO'S LETTERS TO HIS SPIRITUAL DIRECTOR

Edited by
Gianluigi Pasquale

Pauline
BOOKS & MEDIA
Boston

Library of Congress Cataloging-in-Publication Data

Pio, of Pietrelcina, Saint, 1887-1968.
  [Mie stimmate. English]
  Secrets of a soul : Padre Pio's letters to his spiritual director /
edited by Gianluigi Pasquale.
      p. cm.
  ISBN 0-8198-5947-8
  1. Pio, of Pietrelcina, Saint, 1887-1968—Correspondence. 2.
Capuchins—Italy—Correspondence. 3.
Stigmatics—Italy—Correspondence. I. Pasquale, Gianluigi. II. Pio, of
Pietrelcina, Saint, 1887-1968. Vittima per consolare Gesáu. English.
III. Title.
  BX4705.P49 A4 2003
  282'.092—dc22

                                              2003018596

Milan: Edizioni San Paolo, 2002

Printed and published in the U.S.A. by Pauline Books & Media,
50 Saint Pauls Avenue, Boston MA 02130-3491.

www.pauline.org

Pauline Books & Media is the publishing house of the Daughters of St.
Paul, an international congregation of women religious serving the
Church with the communications media.

1 2 3 4 5 6 7   08 07 06 05 04 03

To Giovanna,
whom I love more than anyone else,
because she is forever my mother.
And to Brother Sisto Zarpellon,
who said to me, "If you wish."
From then on, everything has been
so wonderful.
G. P.

Contents

BOOK I

MY STIGMATA

BOOK II

VICTIM TO CONSOLE THE HEART OF JESUS

Introduction

"You are a letter of Christ..." (2 Cor 3:3).

We who have received the grace of believing in Christ, the Revealer of the Father and the Savior of the world, have a duty to show to what depths the relationship with Christ can lead.

The great mystical tradition of the Church of both East and West has much to say in this regard. It shows how prayer can progress, as a genuine dialogue of love, to the point of rendering the person wholly possessed by the divine Beloved, vibrating at the Spirit's touch, resting filially within the Father's heart. This is the lived experience of Christ's promise: "he who loves me will be loved by my Father, and I will love Him and manifest myself to Him" (Jn 14:21). It is a journey totally sustained by grace, which nonetheless demands an intense spiritual commitment and is no stranger to painful purifications (the "dark night"). But it leads, in various possible ways, to the ineffable joy experienced by the mystics as "nuptial union."

These words from Pope John Paul II's apostolic letter, *Novo Millennio Ineunte* (n. 33), best illustrate the intent of this volume of letters of Padre Pio of Pietrelcina, compiled according to themes in order to make them more accessible to an ever growing audience. In these letters, Padre Pio's intense personality clearly emerges, as well as the principal purpose of his existence as a Christian and Capuchin religious: to fill with love and self-sacrifice the gap that exists between God the Creator and those who distance themselves from Him.

Padre Pio is a person who has an almost universal appeal, and by the power and clarity of his religious experience, he urges all souls, through Jesus, to turn toward God and eternal realities. Far more than the mark of the stigmata, his person and message are explicit reminders of the Second Vatican Council's (1962–1965) declaration regarding the "signs of the times." The Council indicated certain points that attest more directly to God's presence in the world and to his plan for the salvation of humanity. The following, in particular, are to be remembered: the personal sanctity of the believer, who gives witness to the news of the Gospel and charity as the earmark of the true disciple of Christ (*Lumen Gentium,* nn. 39–42); the necessity of suffering and the cross as a means to salvation for those who seek peace and justice (*Gaudium et Spes,* n. 38); martyrdom as the supreme sign of love and consistency in one's life (*Lumen Gentium,* n. 42); respect for the dignity of the human person (*Gaudium et Spes,* nn. 63–72); and the search for peace (*Gaudium et Spes,* nn. 77–90).

For those who read the testimony deposed during the process of his canonization, there is no doubt that Padre Pio significantly characterizes twentieth-century holiness precisely because he knew how to reconcile the announcement of the Gospel with the signs of the times enumerated by the Council. It is essentially for this reason that crowds of believers, as well as non-believers and the curious, gather around this Capuchin friar's tomb today. People from the most diverse paths and disparate ideologies find in Padre Pio a source of meaning and direction. His life was marked by the incredible, and yet it outlines a program of Christian living that is possible and accessible to each of us, a program, which, for both believers and non-believers alike, fulfills God's plan that all people come to know the saving truth.

In presenting this volume, first published on the occasion of the canonization of the stigmatic from Gargano, I, together with the curator of the letters, wish to thank in particular the Most Reverend Father Gerardo Di Flumeri, O.F.M. Cap., the tireless and expert vice-postulator of the cause, for having authorized the reproduction of these letters, thus revealing to the public at large this veritable goldmine of spirituality that, in some ways, has only begun to be explored. My hope is those who will read this volume will desire to take some steps in the direction toward becoming better acquainted with the authentic beauty of Padre Pio's life.

BROTHER FLORIO ALESSANDRO TESSARI, O.F.M. CAP.

BOOK I

MY STIGMATA

Foreword

A Man Marked by Love: Sign of the Permanence of Prophecy in the Church

The gift of the stigmata undoubtedly belongs to the prophetic charism that "must remain in all the Church until the final coming."[1] Just as for Francis of Assisi (1181–1226), history's first stigmatic, so too for his cleric Franciscan son, Padre Pio's bodily mark or sign of the stigmata possesses two inseparable features. In the first place, the stigmata bears witness to the fact that in the history of the Church the prophetic gift has not and never will fail. In the second place the stigmata is a clear sign that conversion, is manifested by the most humanly qualifying act of abandonment to God by means of faith.

Those who interpret the stigmata of Padre Pio (1887–1968), as well as that of Francis of Assisi or the Poor Clare nun, St. Veronica Giuliana (1660-1727), do so knowing full well that throughout history God speaks in word and sign. Jesus is the Most High Revealer of God the Father by means of the Holy Spirit, and through the wounds of the nails that fixed Him to the cross and the lance that pierced His side, Jesus initiates this means by which God *marks* the Word Incarnate, fully revealed in his only Son. It is only by the power of God's grace and

---

1. Eusebius of Cesarea, *Historia Ecclesiastica,* V, 17, 4.

mercy that we are marked from the day of our baptism with the sign of our salvation.

If Padre Pio's stigmata are a sign of the prophecy of the New Testament, we should not obscure it beneath an oppressive cloak, focusing on his special gift of foreknowledge of events. Rather, as a sign, it should continue to be for Christians today a word of comfort, trust, and hope.

Padre Pio, a twentieth-century Capuchin friar, passed away shortly after the conclusion of the Second Vatican Council, which, in a real sense, was a prophetic event. For those with the eyes to see and contemplate, the work of the Council allows us to observe the power of faith, hope, and charity present and operative in us.

On the same level as Francis of Assisi and Veronica Giuliani, St. Padre Pio incarnated the Franciscan spirituality. As this collection of his letters clearly attests, he lived the unexpected and difficult gift of the stigmata as a true priest. At thirty-one years of age, having been a priest for eight years and a Capuchin religious for fifteen, Padre Pio received this sign of the love of Jesus crucified, making him the first stigmatic priest thus far in the history of the Church.

Preface

The Crucifix of September 20, 1918

Padre Pio was born in Pietrelcina, a town outside Benevento, Italy, on May 25, 1887. His parents, Grazio Maria Forgi-
one and Maria Giuseppa Di Nunzio brought him to the Church
of St. Mary of the Angels the following day to be baptized. He
was given the name Francis.

On January 22, 1903, Francis entered the novitiate of the
Capuchin monastery in Morcone and changed his name to Pio.
On January 22, 1904, he was admitted to temporary vows,
professing to live poverty, chastity, and obedience. Four years
later, according to the canonical norms observed at the time, he
professed his perpetual profession of vows in the order of Capuchin Friars Minor. Having fulfilled his course of studies in
theology, with a few brief interruptions because of his poor
health, he was ordained a priest in the canons chapel of the
cathedral at Benevento on August 10, 1904. After spending brief
periods in a number of monasteries, he was finally transferred to
the monastery in San Giovanni Rotondo, near Foggia, Italy,
where he remained uninterruptedly for fifty years, until his
death on September 23, 1968.

On September 20, 1918, Padre Pio was physically marked
with the gift of the stigmata. It was a Friday, the day on which
Jesus was crucified. The event took place between the hours of

9:00 and 10:00 A.M. As is clear in his letters, this phenomenon was preceded by a "transverberation" or "invisible stigmata" on his hands and in his side.

On the evening of August 5, 1918, a little more than a month before receiving the physical stigmata, Padre Pio, while hearing confessions, was wounded by a mysterious Being. Struck by a long blade with a tip of fire, he felt the pain that mystics such as St. John of the Cross (1542–1591) defined as the "assault of the Seraphim." Only with difficulty was Padre Pio able to retire to his room, suffering severe pains that lasted until the morning of August 7. He remained in bed in order to hide from everyone the true cause of his suffering. Only later did he reveal that he had been physically wounded in his side.

September 20, 1918 has peculiar historical significance: the massive bloodshed of World War I ended shortly after this date. It also follows the anniversary date, September 14, when Francis of Assisi was marked by the stigmata. On that day in 1224, Francis was alone in prayer on the Mount of the Verna, Tuscany. He asked the Lord for two graces: to feel in his body and soul the agony endured by Jesus on the cross, and to experience in his own heart the immense love that led Jesus to willingly suffer his passion and death for the salvation of humanity. At that very moment, the hands and feet of the *Poverello di Assisi*[2] began to show the nail marks on his hands and a wound to his side.

According to the description found in Padre Pio's first letter, we learn that he experiences the same phenomenon. On the morning of September 20, the monastery was almost empty. The father guardian was at San Marco in Lamis for the prepara-

---

2. Translator's note: *Poverello* or "poor man," is often used as a euphemism for St. Francis of Assisi.

tion of the feast of St. Matthew the Apostle. Brother Nicholas, the begging friar, had gone out on his rounds. Only Padre Pio remained behind. After celebrating Mass, Padre Pio paused to reflect in the silence of the choir while the brothers had gone outside to relax in the courtyard. Perhaps Padre Pio was praying for the victims of the war or of the horrible epidemic of that year; perhaps he was offering himself as a sacrificial victim. We can only imagine his sensitivity to human suffering and his generous willingness to take on other's sufferings.

The empty church, nestled in the deserted mountainous landscape, gave an even greater intensity to Padre Pio's prayer. He knelt in the choir above the entrance to the little church—still visible today. Before him was a crucifix, hung from the balustrade of the narrow choir from which one could see the principal chapel of the presbytery. That cypress wood crucifix, which still hangs in that church today, was carved by an anonymous seventeenth-century artist, who departed from anatomical proportions to give a pained and crude expression to the figure of the dying Christ. Accentuated in red, the blood flowing from the numerous wounds is striking. With eyes open, the crucified Christ is in agony, tormented by pain, and seems to be struggling to find a less excruciating position. Alone at that moment, no one can witness to the facts Padre Pio later related with the documentary rigor of a news report to his spiritual director, Father Benedetto, who required Padre Pio to reveal "every detail, under the oath of holy obedience"; this he did some thirty-two days after the event in a letter dated October 22, 1918.

From the reconstruction of the autobiographical experience that emerges in the letter, it is obvious that Padre Pio exercised an immense effort to adequately express the gift of the stigmata, a difficulty not uncommon among mystics in the face of phenomenon that completely transcend the natural order. However, for the holy man of Gargano, it is possible to delineate the following points. First, Padre Pio was meditating before a wooden crucifix on the passion of Christ, praying intensely to participate in the agonies of the crucifixion so as to "become a second crucifix." Next, he passed into an ecstasy of love during which the image is fused with a "large Being," though nothing further is specified. Then dazzling arrows shoot out from the wounds of the crucifix in the direction of the seer's hands, feet, and side. Finally, at the end of the ecstasy, the holy man becomes aware of his open wounds.

Without a Francis of Assisi
There Would Be No Padre Pio

Concerning the gift of the stigmata, the greatest similarity that can be drawn between Francis of Assisi and Padre Pio revolves, on the one hand, around the complex relationship between the body and the soul, between illness and holiness, and on the other hand, the extraordinary sensibility that characterized both men. With respect to the frequent illnesses that afflicted Francis, especially following his conversion, and Padre Pio, it is particularly noteworthy that both the theological and psychiatric sciences agree that the stigmata are an outstanding language of the body. "The stigmata," writes Umberto Galimberti, "were neither simulations contrived to deceive, nor illnesses that presupposed a cause, but primitive forms of communication for those who did not possess a more evolved means."[3] Above all, to compare Francis of Assisi and Padre Pio means to observe

---

3. *Psichiatria e fenomenologia,* 279.

their extraordinary sensitivity. St. Francis left an indelible mark not only on the religiosity of his historic period, but for all time because of his store of emotions and capacity for poetic expression, as seen in various biographical episodes, such as the Christmas celebration at Greccio, his *Canticle to Brother Sun,* and his brotherly love for all creation. Similarly, from the *Letters* of the holy man from Gargano and the testimony of those who knew him, one encounters Padre Pio's uncommon affectivity and his immense need to be repaid in kind. His affectionate heart is revealed in the ease with which he was moved, frequently to the point of weeping, in "bearing" the passion of Christ and the suffering of others.

The extraordinary sensitivity of both men is also revealed in another unmistakable characteristic: modesty regarding the signs that appeared on their bodies. St. Francis exercised the utmost discretion with respect to all of his spiritual experiences, fearing to risk their effectiveness by showing them to others without having received God's explicit nod of approval. As was his custom, Francis of Assisi drew upon all the resources of his intelligence to keep his wounds hidden even from the inquisitive eyes of those brothers appointed to assist him. No less interesting is the manner in which the holy Padre Pio reacted after having been stigmatized. In his letter dated October 22, 1918, as directed by his spiritual father, Benedetto of San Marco in Lamis (1872–1942), Padre Pio expresses the hope that Jesus will take away the "confusion that I am undergoing because of these external signs." He considers them the cause "of an indescribable and unbearable humiliation." Furthermore, his attitude in other circumstances corresponded to that of Francis. For example, probably not long after the stigmatization, during an informal conversation, Father Nazzareno of Arpaise (1885–

1960) insistently asked to see the wound to his side. "Padre Pio would reply," wrote Father Nazzareno, "with that passage from the book of Tobias: 'It is good to keep hidden the secret of the King'" (12:7). Even Father Paolino of Casacalenda (1886–1964) testifies that after Padre Pio received the stigmata, he would cover the wounds on his hands with gloves and wrap a bandage around the wound to his side.

In the final analysis to view Padre Pio's stigmata as part of the prophetic charism, similar to that of Francis of Assisi, means to realize that the imprint of Christ is profoundly impressed in each baptized person. The mystics understood this perfectly. In fact, they drove themselves to dangerous limits, conceiving a "saintly" Christian as a "secon
d Christ." If this can be said of Francis of Assisi, it is equally valid for Padre Pio, as those with the eyes to read in faith will discover in each of his letters.

GIANLUIGI PASQULAE, O.F.M. CAP.

⸎ *1* ⸎

"It was on the morning of the twentieth last month..."

In this most famous of Padre Pio's letters, he describes the event of the stigmatization to his spiritual director Father Benedetto, the provincial superior of the Capuchins of Sant'Angelo-Foggia at the time. Here there emerges a clear distinction between the phenomenon of transverbation and the subsequent stigmata [510].[4]

San Giovanni Rotondo, October 22, 1918

⸎

J.M.J.D.F.C.[5]

My dearest father,

May Jesus, the Sun of Justice, shine ever brightly on your spirit, enveloped in the mysterious darkness of the trial willed directly by Him!

---

4. The number in brackets indicates the numbering in the complete edition of the *Epistolary,* vol. I, Edizioni Padre Pio da Pietrelcina, San Giovanni Rotondo (Foggia), 2000.

5. These initials, found at the beginning of all of Padre Pio's letters, represent the first letters of the names Jesus, Mary, Joseph, Dominic, Francis, and Clare. At times Padre Pio leaves off the initials for Dominic and Clare. At other times an "I" is used for the initials of Jesus and Joseph, denoting the Latin: Iesus, Iosef.

O father, why are you so distraught and so full of worries over your spirit? Calm yourself because Jesus is with you and is happy with you. It torments my soul to know that you are in so much spiritual suffering. O, how I have prayed and continue to pray for you to our Lord, who makes me feel in my heart that He has always been with you, and that, indeed, He has doubled His graces, His preferences, His predilections toward your soul.

Therefore, how can you allow yourself to be persuaded that the calamities that roar about you are from God and that, in large measure, you are their cause? O father, do not be afraid, I beg you. You are not in the least bit guilty for these howling tempests. You must have no fear for your soul; Jesus is with you and you are most dear to Him. This is the whole truth before God. Calm down and let the Lord test you as He will, because everything shall come to pass for your sanctification.

No, I did not keep silent in my last letter out of a sense of *false pity,* as you reprimanded, or not to advise you on how your soul's impenitence accumulates on your [spirit] as you falsely fear. I kept silent because I did not have the strength to admonish you in that regard. I beg you not to commit a further wrong to divine Goodness by refusing to abandon this false conviction.

According to God's purposes, the current scourge[6] is to draw man to divinity, which is, after all, our principal end; and the secondary or more immediate aim is to exonerate the persecutions against the children of God by other children of God, which is the fruit of this present war.

Do not be afraid, then, that iniquity shall crush decency; that very iniquity shall crush itself and justice shall triumph.

---

6. World War I.

What can I say with regard to your question about how my crucifixion took place? My God, what confusion and humiliation I undergo in having to make known what You, O Lord, did in this wretched creature of Yours!

It was on the morning of the twentieth last month in the choir, after the celebration of the holy Mass, when I was suddenly surprised by stillness as in a sweet slumber. All of my internal and external senses and even the very faculties of my soul were engulfed in an indescribable quiet. In all of this there was a total silence around and within me. There suddenly arose a sense of great peace and abandonment to the complete loss of all things and a peace in the very collapse itself. All this happened in a flash.

And while all this was going on, I saw before me a mysterious Being, like the one I saw on August 5, only now he was bleeding from his hands, feet, and side. Seeing him terrifies me. I cannot tell you what I felt inside at that instant; I felt I was dying, and I would have died had not the Lord intervened to support my heart, which I felt pounding in my chest.

The vision of that Being retreated and I noticed that my hands, feet, and side were pierced and bleeding. Imagine the torment that I experienced then and experience continuously almost every day.

Blood flows steadily from the wound to my heart, especially from Thursday evenings through Saturday.[7] My father, I am dying of pain because of the torment and the confusion that I feel in the depths of my soul. I fear I will bleed to death if the

---

7. In his script, Saturday, or "Sabato" in Italian, is written "sabito"—the Pietrelcina dialect.

Lord does not heed the groans of my poor heart by withdrawing this from me. Will Jesus, who is so good, grant me this grace?

Will He perhaps at least take away the confusion I am experiencing because of these external signs? I will lift up my voice and shout to Him and will not stop beseeching Him until, through His mercy, He withdraws from me not the torment, not the pain—because I think that is impossible and I want to intoxicate myself with pain[8]—but these external marks that are the cause of indescribable and unbearable confusion and humiliation.

The Being about whom I intended to write in my last letter is none other than the same one I wrote of in another letter, the one I saw on August 5. He follows his course without rest and with supreme torment to the soul. I feel a continuous uproar within me like a waterfall that always spews blood. My God! The punishment is fitting, the sentence just, but use me to mercy's end. *Domine,* I will always say with your prophet, *"Domine, ne in furore tuo arguas me, neque in ira tua corripias me!"*[9]

---

8. Padre Pio suffers more from the "humiliation" of the external sign of God's predilection than from the pain caused by the wounds. His desire for pain is not motivated by masochism, but by his belief that this makes him an intimate sharer in Jesus' mission of saving souls. Here we can recall St. Paul's letter to the Colossians (1:24), when he writes, "In my flesh I complete what is lacking in Christ's afflictions for the sake of his body, that is, the Church."

9. Ps 6:2 and 38:1: "O LORD, do not rebuke me in your anger, or discipline me in your wrath."

My father, now that the depths of my being are known to you, do not refuse to let a word of comfort reach me here in the midst of such severe and unyielding bitterness.

I always pray for you, for poor, dear Father Agostino, for everyone.

Bless me always.

Your most affectionate son,

FRA PIO[10]

---

10. Following an authentic Capuchin tradition, Padre Pio always signs his letters "fra," or brother, using the lower case "f."

·❧· *2* ·❧·

"The flames that disturb my heart in these moments…"

For Padre Pio, as many Western and Eastern mystics before him, the spiritual director was an indispensable aid. Padre Pio's revered director, Father Benedetto, contributed much to the spiritual rebirth of the religious men in his province during the first half of the twentieth century. Speaking with the intimacy of a "son" to his "father," Pio opens himself to Benedetto and tells him of the first signs of his direct participation in the passion of Jesus [17].

Pietrelcina, September 4, 1910

·❧·

J.M.J.F.

My dearest father,

As is God's will, I continue to suffer ill health even now. But what torments me the most are the strong, acute pains in my thorax. At times the pains trouble me so much that I feel as if my back and chest will split. Yet, Jesus never fails to assuage my suffering, from time to time, by speaking to my heart. O yes, my father, how good Jesus is to me! O what precious moments these are! It is a happiness I can liken to nothing else, a happiness that the Lord gives me to relish almost only in moments of affliction.

At these moments, more than ever, when the whole world troubles and weighs on me, I desire nothing other than to love and to suffer.[11] Yes, my father, even in the midst of so much suffering I am happy because it seems as if my heart is beating with Jesus' heart. You can only imagine how much delight is infused in a heart that knows, almost with certainty, that it possesses Jesus.

It is true that the temptations I am subjected to are very many indeed, but I trust Divine Providence will not to let me fall into the tempter's snares. It is also true that quite often Jesus hides Himself, but what does that matter; with your help I will try to remain close to Him, having your assurance that I am not abandoned but merely toyed with by Love.

O, how I long for someone to help me temper my anxieties and the flames that disturb my heart at these moments.

Please do me the charity of responding—if you wish and if it is not a bother. Please assure me of the truth in what I have thus far revealed to you.

I ask that you commend me to the Lord and bless me.

Yours,

FRA PIO

I send my regards, my thanks, and my best wishes to the lector, Father Agostino, for all the good that he has done for me.

---

11. Padre Pio reflects a profound understanding of his Christian and religious call to daily live the Paschal mystery in his own being, and thus to participate in the salvific mission of Jesus. He does not desire suffering in and for itself but only insofar as it unites him intimately with Jesus and allows him to share in Christ's mission.

"I will not tire of praying to Jesus."

The distinct Franciscan characteristic by which Padre Pio draws near to the "mysteries of humanity" of the Son of God is evident in this third letter. The particular message that emerges here is that Padre Pio is convinced that he dwells safely in the arms of Jesus, and that the demon wants to tear him from that embrace. Pio is convinced that Jesus does not want to lose "His fra Pio," because He did not measure the blood He shed on the cross for the salvation of all humanity [25].

Pietrelcina, December 20, 1910

~

J.M.J.F.

My dearest father,

Blessed Christmas draws near, and it seems a duty of conscience compels me not to allow the time to pass without wishing you a Christmas full of all the heavenly consolations your heart desires. Though I pray at all times for you, whom I love dearly, during these days I will not fail to double my prayers to the heavenly Child, so that He might condescend to keep you from every earthly misfortune, most especially from the ill fortune of losing the infant Jesus.

My ill health continues on its course of ups and downs. It is true I am suffering, and suffering a great deal, but I am also most delighted, because in the midst of my suffering the Lord allows me to feel inexpressible joy.

My father, if it were not for the strife that the demon continuously stirs up within me I would almost be in Paradise. I find myself in the hands of the demon, who is struggling to tear me from the arms of Jesus. My God, what battles he stirs within me! Sometimes it is all I can do to hold on to my senses because of the constant violence I must inflict on myself. My father, how many tears and sighs I address to heaven asking to be liberated from this toil. But it does not matter; I will not tire of praying to Jesus. It is true that my prayers are more worthy of punishment than reward because I have displeased Jesus with my innumerable sins.[12] But in the end He will either be moved to pity me and take me from this world and call me to His side, or He will liberate me from this toil. And if He chooses not to grant me either of these graces, I hope that He will at least continue to grant me the grace not to succumb to temptation. Jesus did not measure the blood He shed for the salvation of humanity, could He possibly measure my sins in order to lose me? I do not

_____

12. This is a rather common exaggeration in Catholic hagiography, which has roots in a profound and intimate knowledge of human weakness and divine holiness. These and other similar expressions of Padre Pio are authoritatively proven wrong by Father Benedetto.

believe so. With faithfulness, He will soon vindicate Himself with His holy love for this most disagreeable of His creatures.

And what do you say about all this? Please tell Jesus that I will keep my promise not to displease Him anymore and, instead, I will strive to love Him always.

Bless me, as I am your humble,

FRA PIO

I need a cincture. I commend myself to your charity.

❦ 4 ❦

"Jesus is with me, so what can I possibly fear?"

Here we have an excellent detailed analysis in which Padre Pio describes for Father Benedetto the temptations of the Evil One. These temptations distance him from living the present moment and take him back in memory to past faults, which have already been forgiven. This causes Padre Pio to become downhearted, almost depressed. Praying at the feet of Jesus, he feels comforted and refreshed in the continuous struggle to overcome the temptations that bring him back "to the secular life" [30].

Pietrelcina, March 19, 1911

❦

J.M.J.F.

My dearest father,

On the occasion of your name day, and heeding the voice in my heart that tells me to be grateful to my superior and father, I send you this letter to wish you the happiest name day ever.

On this day I will not fail to redouble my prayers to the Lord, so He might grant to keep you from every misfortune.

My father, the demon continues to stir up strife within me and, unfortunately, gives no indication of being beaten. When I was first put to the test—I confess my weakness—I was melancholy, but then, little by little, this melancholy passed and I began to feel a bit comforted. Praying at the feet of Jesus, I seem not to feel at all the weight of the struggle or the bitterness of the sorrows I undergo in order to gain the upper hand whenever I am tempted.

The temptations that concern my secular life are such that they touch my heart, darken my mind, cause me to break into a cold sweat, and, I would even say, make me tremble from head to foot. At such moments, all that remains are my eyes for weeping, and I comfort and encourage myself only by thinking of the suggestions you gave me in your letters.

Even going to the altar—my God!—I feel such assaults! But Jesus is with me, so what can I possibly fear?

Bless me profoundly, and do not fail to commend me to Jesus, as I do you every day.

Your,

FRA PIO

"It seems impossible that Jesus wants me to be lost."

Padre Pio knows that sin creates a dramatic rupture between God and the sinner, and that anyone, including himself, is capable of falling into this abyss. Yet, Padre Pio also believes that God has placed everything, including judgment, into the hands of the Son. The Father has "given all judgment" to Him (Jn 5:22). For this reason Padre Pio sees that it is impossible that God would permit him to be lost [42].

San Marco la Catola, September 5, 1911

◌·

W.J.M.J.F.[13]

Dear father,

Jesus continues to be with me and He has not left me yet, thus the increased ease with which I resist temptations and resign myself to the divine will as I already wrote in my last letter. You see then, father, to what point God's goodness and sweetness abounds despite however wicked I may be!

---

13. Translator's note: There is no explanation offered in the original text for the meaning of the initial "W." Without a period, "W" is used in modern Italian to stand for *Evviva* meaning "Hurray for" or, and perhaps more appropriately here, "Long live…" or "Praise be…." The fact that Padre Pio begins Letter 8 with the exclamation *viva Gesù* ("Long live Jesus!") may be an indication of his intent here.

And what can I do to correspond to so much mercy? What can I give Him in return for so many blessings? If you only knew how many times in the past I exchanged Jesus for some vile object of this world! I see a mystery in me; I continually regret the sins I have committed, continually propose never to commit them again, continually declare my resolute will never to sin again. Yet, with bloodshot eyes, I am sorry to say that notwithstanding all of this, I am still so imperfect, and it seems to me that very often I displease the Lord. At times I am overcome by great desperation because it seems almost impossible that Jesus must pardon my many sins. However, more often than not it seems impossible to me that Jesus wants me to be lost. What is this? Please explain this to me a little. Yet, all of this happens to me without my noticing, for I in no way will to displease God, even slightly.

How I suffer, father, seeing that Jesus is not only ignored by men but, what is worse, He is insulted and, above all, with horrible blasphemies. I would rather die or at least become deaf than hear the many insults men address to God.

I offered the following prayer to the Lord: Lord, let me die rather than find myself in the company of those who offend you! I commend you to the Lord also, and I ask that He grant me this grace if it is for His greater glory.

I finished celebrating the Gregorian Masses. Now I beg you to send me a few alms, because presently the lack of funds prevents me from procuring my medications.

Do not cease to bless me always.

Your,

FRA PIO

6

"In the middle of the palms of my hands, there appeared a small red spot."

This letter is an example of the delicate trust that existed between the 24-year-old Padre Pio and his spiritual director. With profound intimacy, Pio opens his heart and tells of all that has been happening to him for more than a year. Only those who live the rich silence of love in a Franciscan cloister can understand the profound act of faith that "fra Pio" makes in confessing, full of modesty and "shame," the first signs of his transverberation [44].

Pietrelcina, September 8, 1911

·◇·

J.M.J.F.

My dear father,

Do not chastise me for being a bit late in answering your last letter. It was not due to a lack of good will or laziness, but for the reason that I was in the country in order to breathe some healthier air, after which I experienced an improvement [to my health]. Therefore, upon returning to town to celebrate Mass—today in fact—your letter was handed to me and I was determined to answer it without losing any time.

Last night something happened, something I cannot explain or comprehend. In the middle of the palms of my hands, there appeared a little red spot, almost the size of a coin, accompanied by a strong, sharp pain at the center of the red spots. The pain was more intense in my left hand, so much so that I still feel it aching. I also notice some pain in my feet.

This phenomenon has been occurring for nearly a year, though there was a brief time when it did not occur. Please do not become impatient with me if this is only the first time I am telling you—until now I always allowed myself to be overcome by a cursed shame. If you only knew the violence I must inflict upon myself even now to tell you about it! I would have told you many things, but I lacked the words. I will only tell you that my heart beats very strongly when I am with the sacramental Jesus. At times it seems that my heart will come right out of my chest.

At the altar I sometimes feel my entire body burning; I cannot even describe it to you. In particular, my face seems to be going up in flames. What these signs mean, my father, I do not know.

You can only imagine then how much it is my wish to return to the monastery.[14] The greatest of sacrifice that I have offered the Lord is precisely that of not being able to live in the monastery. I cannot believe that God absolutely wants me to die. It is true that I have and am suffering at home, but this has never rendered me powerless of fulfilling my office,[15] something that was never possible in the monastery. If it is a matter of having to suffer alone, so be it. But being a burden and cause of

---

14. Padre Pio is forced by a severe illness to return to his family.

15. This "office" is the celebration of the Mass. Strangely, the illness that afflicts Padre Pio persists only in the monastery, making it impossible for him to celebrate the Eucharist within walls.

anxiety for others to no other end than my death leaves me speechless. After all, it seems to me that I have the right and duty not to deprive myself of life at the age of 24! It seems to me the Lord does not want that. Consider that I am more dead than alive, and then do as you believe you must. I am ready to make any sacrifice if it is a matter of obedience.

Thank you for the cassock. I will say the five masses for August and the five for September during the course of this month and at the beginning of the next.

As I await your response, I ask your blessing.

Your,

FRA PIO

"The consolations are so soothing that they cannot be described."

The letters of Padre Pio describe his spiritual program and interior life. In all of the letters, but above all in this one, there are three consistent characteristics: a constant reference to Jesus, a promise to pray for his spiritual director and his other acquaintances, and an affirmation of the continual interferences of the Evil One, here called "barbablù"[16] by Padre Pio [71].

Pietrelcina, March 31, 1912

∽·

J.M.J.F.

My dearest father,

Mindful of the great care shown me, and now that the holy season of Easter is approaching,[17] I feel a sacred duty not to let this time go by without wishing you an Easter full of all the graces that can make you happy here on earth and blessed in heaven.

---

16. Translator's note: *Barbablù* may be translated as "bluebeard," perhaps referring to the ruthless character of the well-known folk tale.

17. In 1912 Easter fell on April 7.

This, my father, is my wish for you, and I believe that you will find it most welcome. On this solemnity, I will not fail, in my unworthiness, to pray to the resurrected Jesus for your beautiful soul—though I do not forget to pray for you every day.

More than ever during these holy days, I am afflicted by that *barbablù*. I pray, therefore, that you strongly commend me to the Lord, so that He will not leave me victim to this common enemy.

However, God is with me, and the consolations He allows me to relish always are so sweet that they cannot be described.

I am feeling fairly well. I imagine that you are not content with this general description of my internal state, but, my father, the apparition deprives me even of the ability to narrate this to you in minute detail. God knows how much violent shaking it causes me after writing only a bit.

Until we meet again, my father, when and where God wills, I kiss your hand and I pray that you will earnestly bless me.

Your,

FRA PIO, CAPUCHIN

༒ 8 ༒

"The heart of Jesus and my heart were fused."

One must read this letter remembering that the author is only 25 years old. God is progressively assimilating the young man to Himself through the union of two hearts: the divine and human heart of the Savior and Padre Pio's heart, awash with such sweetness. The description of this union is sketched out in terms of a conversation between the two hearts in the prayer of thanksgiving offered after the Eucharist. Beginning with this letter, the addressee is no longer Father Benedetto, but Father Agostino, Padre Pio's new spiritual director [74].

Pietrelcina, April 18, 1912

༒

J.M.J.F.

My dearest *babbo*,[18]

Long live Jesus! I am most delighted to be able to spend some time with you via this letter. But how can I possibly tell you about Jesus' new triumphs over my soul during the last few days? I will abstain [limit] myself to telling you about what

---

18. Translator's note: This is a common term of endearment used for one's father. In the original Italian, Padre Pio addresses Father Benedetto as *padre* ("father"), whereas he addresses Father Agostino (cf. Letter 8ff.) as *babbo*, which has no English equivalent to reflect the emotional nuance.

happened to me last Tuesday.[19] What a burning fire I felt in my heart on that day! But I also felt that this fire had been ignited by a friendly and divinely jealous hand.

I was still in bed when I was visited by those *foul creatures* that strike me in such a barbaric manner that I considered it a very great grace to have been able to endure it without dying—a trial, my *babbo,* which was far superior to my strength.

Afterward the good Jesus, who permitted the *barbablù* to treat me in that way, did not fail to console and fortify my soul.

I was barely able to go to the divine Prisoner to celebrate Mass, but when it was over, I stayed a while with Jesus in order to give thanks for His graces. O how gentle was the conversation that I had with Paradise that morning! Even if I wanted to try to tell everything, I would not be able to. Things were said that cannot be translated into human language without losing their deep and celestial meaning. The heart of Jesus and my heart were, if you will permit the expression, fused. They were not two hearts beating, but one. My heart had disappeared as a drop of water in the ocean. Jesus was Paradise, King. My joy was so intense and profound that I could contain myself no longer and the most delightful tears flowed down my face.

Yes, my *babbo,* human beings cannot understand that when Paradise pours itself into a heart, this afflicted, exiled, weak, and mortal heart cannot bear it without weeping. Yes, I repeat, the joy that filled my heart was such that it made me weep at length.

Believe me, this visitation encouraged me completely. Long live the divine Prisoner!

---

19. That is, April 16, 1912. The mystical phenomenon called "fusion of hearts" is described.

The demon will make it impossible for us to see each other before the chapter meeting, but it does not matter if he succeeds in preventing us from embracing. From this moment I will make a sacrifice of this to Jesus. We will behold one another before Jesus.

I end here because I am exhausted and cannot go on any longer.

When you are before Him [the Blessed Sacrament], do not forget to put in a good word for your humble disciple.

FRA PIO

My family, the archpriest,[20] and all our friends send you their best.

---

20. A title similar to Monsignor.

"My father, I feel that love will ultimately conquer me."

The feast of San Lorenzo, August 10, reminds Padre Pio of the anniversary of his priestly ordination. Though eight years have already passed, he does not forget the very real sense of peace his heart began to experience on the day of his ordination. It is a peace that never abandoned him because, day after day, love for Jesus inundated every inch of his intellectual, moral, and spiritual stature [93].

Pietrelcina, August 9, 1912

∽

J.M.J.F.

Dearest *babbo,*

I have wanted to write for some time, but *barbablù* prevented me from doing so. I say that he prevented me because every time I was determined to write you, I was assailed by a very strong headache, which made me feel as if my head were about to split then and there. This was accompanied by a very sharp pain to my right arm, which made it impossible for me to hold a pen.

My father, I feel that love will ultimately conquer me. My soul runs the risk of dividing itself from my body because it cannot love Jesus enough on this earth.

Yes, my soul is wounded by love for Jesus. I am crippled with love. I continually experience the bitter pain of a fierce fire that burns and does not consume. Suggest to me, if you can, some remedy for this current condition of my soul.

Here is a pale image of what Jesus is doing within me: Just as a stream drags along to the depths of the sea all it encounters on its course, so my soul, which has sunk into the shoreless ocean of Jesus' love, without any merit on my part and without my understanding why, draws with it all His treasures.

My father, while I am writing my mind wanders off to the beautiful day of my ordination. Tomorrow is the Feast of San Lorenzo, which is also my feast day. I have already begun to experience again the joy of that sacred day. Since this morning I have begun to savor Paradise.... What will it be like when we savor it eternally? I compare the peace I felt in my heart on that day with the peace I feel in my heart, and I find no difference.

The feast of San Lorenzo was the day on which I found my heart ignited by the love of Jesus. How happy I was, and how I enjoyed that day!

Father, read this letter, and, since I have no doubt that you love me, also pray and thank Jesus for me.

Toward the second half of this month I will need some applications.[21] I would be most grateful if you would ask Father Master[22] if he would provide some for me—if that is not too much trouble for you. It does not matter; Jesus will take care of it.

---

21. Padre Pio refers to some form of topical medication.

22. Tommaso da Montesantangelo.

All your acquaintances send you greetings, the archpriest sends his regards, and I embrace you tenderly.

Your humble disciple,

FRA PIO

≈ *10* ≈

"I felt my heart being wounded by an arrow of fire."

The story of Padre Pio's stigmata can be pieced together from his letters. Late one Friday in August 1912, Padre Pio is mystically wounded in the heart by a flame of blazing fire. In his account to Father Agostino, it appears that this is not a completely new phenomenon to him. He confesses that "I have felt many such transports of love," and offers a correct interpretation of this flame [95].

Pietrelcina, August 26, 1912

≈

J.M.J.F.

Dearest *babbo,*

I lovingly send you best wishes for your approaching name day. Measure it by the love and respect in which your son and disciple holds you. On that day my supplications to the most gentle Jesus will be doubled.

Listen now to what happened to me last Friday.[23] I was in church offering my thanksgiving after Mass when I suddenly felt my heart being wounded by an arrow of fire so sharp and intense that I thought I would die.

---

23. August 23, 1912.

I cannot find the words to help you to understand the intensity of that flame; I am completely powerless to express myself. Can you believe it? My soul, the victim of these consolations, becomes dumb. It seemed to me that I was being entirely immersed into fire by an invisible force... My God, what fire! What sweetness!

I have felt many such transports of love, and, for a while, I remain outside this world. On other occasions, however, the fire was less intense. Instead, this time, a moment, an instant, a second longer, and my soul would have separated from my body...it would have gone to Jesus.

O what a beautiful thing to be a victim of love. How is my soul presently? *Mon cher père, à présent Jésus a retiré son javelot de feu, mais la blessure est mortelle...*[24]

Do not imagine, however, that *barbablù* leaves me alone. I will leave you to imagine the torments he inflicts on my heart according to the degree of divine consolations my soul enjoys. But long live the most gentle Jesus, who gives me the strength to deride that *ugly creature* to its face.

I give thanks to God for the alms of the Masses that you sent me.

As for the gathering for the Rosary, I spoke to the representative of the feast and he was quite grieved to be unable to please me. He has already invited another religious. In the event that this person does not accept, you will be the preferred choice. Dear father, *barbablù* will call up all his diabolical trickery to prevent us from seeing one another again. But may the divine will always be done.

---

24. Translator's note: These lines translated from the French are rendered: *My dear father, at present Jesus has withdrawn his lance of fire, but the wound is mortal.* It is not clear why Padre Pio writes in French at this point.

I send along the greetings and best wishes of all our good friends, together with those of the archpriest.

Je vous salue et vous embrasse, père consolateur.

Votre pauvre,[25]

FRA PIO

---

25. Translator's note: These closing lines are translated as: *I send you my regards and I embrace you, father consoler. Your humble f. Pio.*

✧ 11 ✧

"Jesus allowed my heart to hear His voice."

Conscious that all earthly existence is from God and must return to God, Padre Pio hopes that his life will go by as quickly as "light spreads." He does not shrink from the responsibility of working out his salvation in the time allotted to him by God. Rather, he knows that while on earth an ever-present possibility exists: he could lose Jesus at an instant because his wounded human nature could make a deliberate choice to sin [111].

Pietrelcina, December 29, 1912

✧

I.M.I.F.

My dearest father,

Yet another year is going into eternity carrying the weight of the offences I committed during its course. How many souls more fortunate than I greeted its dawn but not its end! How many souls have entered the house of Jesus, there to remain forever. How many very happy souls I envied have passed into eternity after dying the death of the righteous: kissed by Jesus, comforted by the Sacraments, assisted by a minister of God, heaven's smile on their lips notwithstanding the torment of the physical pains that oppressed them!

Life here below, my father, is a sorrow for me. Living the life of an exile is such a bitter torment that I can hardly bear it. The thought that I could lose Jesus at any instant causes me such anxiety that I cannot express it. Only the soul that sincerely loves Jesus would know how.

In these most solemn days when we celebrate the heavenly Child, I am often overcome by such a surfeit of divine Love that my poor heart pines so. Having fully understood Jesus' condescension toward me, I turned to Him with more confidence in my usual prayer: "O Jesus, if only I could love you and suffer for you as much as I would like, to make you happy and redress in some way humanity's ingratitude toward you!"

Jesus allowed me to hear His voice more strongly in my heart: "My son, love is known in sorrow; you will feel it sharply in your spirit and even more sharply in your body." The meaning of these words, my father, remains obscure to me.

Those *foul creatures* try to torment me in every possible way. For this reason I raise my protests to Jesus and I hear Him repeating to me: "Courage, for after the battle, there will be peace." He says that I need loyalty and love. I am ready for anything in order to do His will. Only pray, I beseech you, that I spend whatever little life is left to me for His glory, and that He allows this time to go by in the same way that light spreads.

I prayed to Jesus about the assignment, which you recently entrusted to my prayers, but He has not answered me. It has been a while since He has granted me an answer to what concerns the business of our province because He is quite displeased by our behavior. Still, it seems to me that you should always promptly accept the burdens imposed on you. Though I think you are rather weak for this office, you should nevertheless accept, because there is a shortage of suitable personnel for the task. I beg you, however, not to seek, not even indirectly, this burden yourself. And if it is at all possible for you to refuse, do so.

I have not received anything from Father Stefano—that is from Foggia. And I have enough of the application until around the middle of next month. After that, God will provide.

I will stop here because I cannot go on. On behalf of the archpriest, my family, and all our good friends, I wish you a happy New Year, and pray that you will extend this to the whole community.

You have me always as your disciple,

FRA PIO

∾ *12* ∾

"Jesus offered this chalice to me yet again."

Spiritual direction was an effective means toward sanctification and a moral support amid the multiple trials Padre Pio endured. It was also a sure guarantee against the possibility of illusions. Oppressed by further apparitions of those "foul creatures" that try to deter him from fulfilling his vow of obedience, Padre Pio speaks against them and, consequently, is battered by them. From the letter we also gather that he has probably been asked to become a teacher for the Capuchin novices. Jesus, the Man of Sorrows, speaks to Padre Pio and invites him to take up the chalice of the passion [114].

Pietrelcina, February 1, 1913

∾

I.M.I.F.

Dearest *babbo*,

Can it be true that I am in the arms of Jesus and that He is mine and that I am completely His? All too often this is the question that spontaneously comes to my lips.

Just recently when I received your letter and before I opened it, those *foul creatures* told me to tear it up or to throw it in the fire. If I had done so, they would have retreated forever and would have no longer molested me.

I did not say a word. I did not give them any sort of answer, all the while scorning them in my heart. So they added, "We want this as a condition for our retreat. In doing this, you do it without contempt for anyone." I answered them saying that nothing would have derailed me from my purpose.

They flung themselves on me as ravenous tigers, cursing me and threatening to make me pay for this answer. My father, they kept their word! From that day on they beat me daily. But I do not fear; have I not a Father in Jesus? Is it not true that I will always be His child? I can say with certainty that Jesus has never forgotten me, even when I was far from Him. He follows me everywhere with His love.

The wish that you expressed on my behalf cannot be fulfilled because it would require two miracles. For one, Jesus, with His grace, would have to do violence to not one but many human freedoms. You already understand what I am saying. I beg of you, therefore, do not be misled into praying for the goal you expressed in your letter. Let us not force, dear father, our mutual promise.

Jesus tells me that in moments of love it is He who pleases me, and it is I who please Him in moments of sorrow. So, to desire health would mean searching for my own joy and not to comfort Jesus. Yes, I love the cross, the cross alone. I love it because I always see it behind Jesus' shoulders. Jesus knows very well by now that my whole life, my entire heart is dedicated completely to Him and to His sorrows.

For pity's sake, my father, bear with me if I continue speaking in this manner. Jesus alone understands what pain awaits me when the sorrowful scene of Calvary is made ready before me. Likewise, the comfort one can give to Jesus not only in bearing His sorrows with Him and when He finds a soul, who, for the love of Him, asks not for consolations but to participate in His very sorrows is incomprehensible.

When Jesus wants me to understand that He loves me, He allows me to savor the wounds, the thorns, the agonies of His passion… When He wants to delight me, He fills my heart with that spirit which is all fire; He speaks to me of His delights. But when He wants to be delighted, He speaks to me of His sorrows, He invites me—with a voice full of both supplication and authority—to affix my body [to the cross] in order to alleviate His suffering.

Who can resist Him? I realize how much my miseries have caused Him to suffer, how much I have caused Him to weep because of my ingratitude, how much I have offended Him. I desire no other than Jesus alone, I want nothing more than His pains (because this is what Jesus' wishes). Let me say—since no one can hear me—I am disposed to remain forever deprived of the sweetness Jesus allows me to feel. I am ready to suffer Jesus hiding His beautiful eyes from me, so long as He does not hide His love from me, because then I would die. But I do not feel I can be deprived of suffering—for this I lack strength.

Perhaps I have not yet expressed myself clearly with regard to the secret of this suffering. Jesus, the Man of Sorrows, wants all Christians to imitate Him; He has offered this chalice to me yet again, and I have accepted it. That is why He does not spare me. My humble sufferings are worth nothing, but Jesus delights in them because He loved [suffering] on earth. Therefore, on certain days when He suffered greatly on earth, He allows me to feel my sufferings even more.

Now shouldn't this alone be enough to humiliate me, to make me seek to be hidden from the eyes of men, since I was made worthy of suffering with Jesus and as Jesus?

Ah, my father! I feel too keenly my ingratitude toward God's majesty.

Regarding that business about which you so urged me, Jesus continues to be closed to me. Every time I turn to that subject, it seems to me that He is very displeased. Let us adore this well deserved punishment in silence! You, in particular, fear not, stay calm.

You gave me the greatest pleasure in transcribing and translating that sonnet.

I send greetings from the archpriest, my family, and Francesco. Pray for him who desires your well-being.

[FRA PIO]

❧ *13* ❧

"Nothing can prevail against those who groan under the weight of the cross."

Padre Pio's correspondence often speaks of his experience of the divine Spouse, the Son of God. The emerging theological undercurrent adheres perfectly to Sacred Scripture and the Tradition of the Church. This is evident in the following letter, in which Jesus calls Padre Pio to bear the cross as a true sign of being a Christian [116].

Pietrelcina, February 13, 1913

❧

I.M.I.F.

Dearest *babbo,*

I find myself content enough. Jesus does not cease desiring my good, notwithstanding my unworthiness, because He does not cease permitting me to be all the more afflicted by those ugly attacks. It has now been twenty-two consecutive days since Jesus has allowed them to vent their fury upon me. My father, my entire body is bruised because of the many blows I have endured till now at the hand of our enemies.

More than once they have come to the point of stripping me of my nightshirt and beating me in that condition. Now tell me, was it not Jesus who helped me—I who am deprived of all others—at those most distressing moments when the demons tried to destroy and ruin me? Add to this the fact that even after they left me, I remained undressed for a long time, being completely powerless to move in the cold of this harsh season. How many other evils would those creatures have unleashed on me if our most gentle Jesus had not helped me!

I do not know what will happen to me. I only know one thing for certain: the Lord will never fall short of His promises. Jesus keeps repeating, "Do not fear, I will make you suffer, but I will also give you strength. I wish your soul to be tried and purified through this daily and hidden martyrdom. Do not be frightened if I permit the demon to torment you, the world to displease you, the people you hold most dear to afflict you, because nothing can prevail against those who, for love of Me, groan under the weight of the cross."

A short while ago Jesus said to me, "How many times would you have abandoned me, my son, if I had not crucified you. Beneath the cross one learns to love, and I do not give this to everyone, but only to those souls who are dearest to me."

I also give thanks to you for the many prayers you offer up to the Lord for me. I promise, when I am with Him, to plead your cause. Jesus is good, and He will not be able to refuse my cries, however weak they may always be.

I have not forgotten to commend those two souls to Jesus. Reassure them, I pray, to remain calm. Jesus requires of them a little more surrender and trust in Him. They, poor souls, do not realize how at such moments they are dearer in His eyes than when they find themselves consoled. They do not perceive it, but they are helped by Jesus more now than before. Jesus wants to win them to Himself alone, and that is why He scatters wide their life of thorns.

When you go to San Marco please give my regards to father provincial. I also desire that you ask him once more if he would authorize me to hear confessions. I am almost certain to be a failure, but I cannot stifle within me this mysterious voice. I am disposed to all that the superior wills, and one more refusal equals a great submission for me.

My whole family sends you greetings. The archpriest sends his regards. Francesco sends you a thousand kisses.

Pray for him who holds you close to his heart.

FRA PIO

"I am loyal. No creature will be lost without knowing it."

In this letter, Padre Pio once again takes up his correspondence with Father Benedetto, his first spiritual director. He writes whatever Jesus suggests he put on paper. The veracity of the content is manifested in the profound prophetic meaning, tinged with revelations, which do not sow dread but hope [136].

Pietrelcina, July 7, 1913

·◇·

J.M.J.D.F.C.

My dearest father,

Benedictus Deus, qui fecit mirabilia solus.[26]

How often I have remembered you and your crosses during these days. Since your last letter, when I found how perplexed you were in spirit, I have not ceased to commend you to the most gentle Jesus with the greatest insistence.

This business of yours kept me in distress until this morning, because the blessed Jesus did not wish to pay attention to me. But, may His infinite goodness be always blessed, He was moved to pity for this poor little wretch!

---

26. Ps 72:18: "Blessed be the LORD…who alone does wondrous things."

Jesus talking

This morning after Mass, while I was completely saddened by the aforementioned business, I was suddenly overcome by so violent a headache that right then and there it seemed impossible to continue with my thanksgiving.

This condition increased my torment. A great aridity of spirit even took possession of me, and who knows what would have happened if what I am about to relate had not taken place.

Our Lord appeared to me and spoke thus: "My child, do not fail to write what you hear from my lips today so that you will not forget. I am loyal; no creature will be lost without knowing it. Very different is light from darkness. I always draw to myself the soul with whom I am accustomed to speaking. Instead, the demon's art is to distance the soul from Me. I never raise dread in the soul that has distanced itself from Me; The demon never places a fear in the soul that moves it closer to Me.

"When I am the author of the fear a soul feels for its eternal health at some moments of life, it is recognizable by the peace and serenity it leaves in the soul…"

This vision and locution of our Lord immersed my soul in such peace and contentment that all the sweetness of the world seemed dull in comparison with a single drop of this beatitude.

Every fear regarding your spirit was immediately dispelled from my mind, and even though trying to me, I felt that similar doubts cannot have power over the soul. I remain very comforted and happy in such good company. And who could say how much help it is for me to have Jesus continually by my side. This makes me think twice about doing something that would displease God. It seems to me that Jesus is constantly watching over me. If it happens that sometimes I lose God's presence, at once I hear our Lord calling me back to my duty. I do not know how to describe the voice with which He calls me back, but I do know it is most penetrating and the soul that hears it can hardly refuse to respond.

Do not ask me, my father, how I am certain that it is our Lord who shows Himself to me, since I do not see with the eyes of my body or my spirit. I do not know. I cannot add more than what I have already said. I only know that He who is at my right is our Lord and none other, and even before He spoke it was firmly impressed in my mind that it was He.

This grace has produced much good in me. My soul is continually engulfed by a great peace. I feel myself powerfully consumed by an extremely great desire to please God. Since the Lord favored me with this grace I look with immense disdain upon everything that does not help me to move toward God. I feel an inexpressible confusion in my inability to understand why such good comes to me.

My soul is spurred on by the liveliest gratitude to attest that the Lord grants such grace to my soul without my meriting it. Far be it for me to consider myself superior to other souls for this reason. On the contrary, I believe that of all the people in the world, I am the one who serves the Lord the least, and since the Lord gave such clarity to my soul through this grace, I acknowledge myself to be more obliged than any other soul to serve and love the Creator.

For my soul, every minute imperfection I commit is a sword of sorrow that pierces my heart. Sometimes I am compelled to exclaim with the Apostle—though, alas, not with the same perfection: "It is no longer I who live,"[27] but I feel someone is within me.

---

27. Gal 2:20.

The other effect of this grace is that life itself is becoming a cruel torment for me. I find comfort only in resigning myself to live for the love of Jesus, though alas, my father, even in this comfort my pain is sometimes intolerable, because my soul desires all of my life to be sown with crosses and persecution.

Natural actions such as eating, drinking, sleeping, weigh upon me greatly. In this condition my soul groans because hours go by too slowly. At the end of each day my soul feels unburdened of a great weight and is very relieved. But then at once my soul feels itself falling into a deeper sadness at the thought that many more days of exile have been set aside for it. At just such moments my soul is led to cry out: "O life, how cruel you are to me! How long you are! O life that is no longer life but torment for me! O death, I know not who can fear you when for you life opens!"

Before the Lord favored me with this grace, the sorrow of my sins, the pain I felt at seeing the Lord so offended, the fullness of emotions I experienced for God in my heart were not so intense as to make me lose control. Still, at times, when this sorrow seems intolerable, and I am unable to stop myself, I am forced to unburden myself in shrill cries. After this grace, my sorrow becomes even rawer so as to seem to me that my heart is being pierced through from one side to the other.

Now it seems that I might penetrate the truth concerning the torment that our most beloved Mother underwent, something not possible for me previously. O, if only men could penetrate the truth concerning this martyrdom! Who would succeed in suffering with this most dear co-redemptrix of ours? Who would refuse her the beautiful title of "Queen of martyrs"?

The thought of death does not frighten me at all, and yet, considering that the greatest saints trembled at its approach, I feel my blood turn to ice in my veins because I think that this is the climax of my blindness, justly permitted by God for my innumerable infidelities.

I clearly realize that I have done nothing for the glory of God, nothing for the well-being of souls. On the contrary, I have done a great deal of damage with my scandalous life. I finally acknowledge that I have done nothing except to have so often harmed myself. O my father, do not believe that it is humility that dictates such language, O no, it is the truth, it is the evidence.

I would like you to also show this letter to father lector[28] who is with you during this month. I beg you, examine what I have written here, and should you find in it some trick of the demon, do not spare me for fear of disheartening me. This thought makes me tremble. I do not want to be a victim of the demon's deceptions.

This brings me to asking a favor of you: I would like this letter to be destroyed along with my two preceding letters. Bear in mind that it was only with this hope that I managed to open myself to you with such trust. This is, after all, a simple desire, which I submit to your goodness for approval. But if you do not find my desire just, I implore you not to let my letters be read by anyone.

I end by asking your paternal blessing. May Jesus fill you with all those graces that I ask of Him for you, and may He always hold His hand full of blessings over you.

Your humble,

FRA PIO, CAPUCHIN

---

28. Father Agostino of San Marco in Lamis.

❧ 15 ❧

"I have great desires to serve God with perfection."

Padre Pio recalls a dialogue with Father Benedetto during the first years after his ordination. In this long letter, Padre Pio illustrates three principal effects of "heavenly favors": an admirable knowledge of God; a clear, humble perception of oneself; and a healthy disdain for earthly things. It is evident that these effects indicate the work of supernatural grace in a creature that believes, and, thus, lives his faith out daily [154].

Pietrelcina, November 1, 1913

❧

J.M.J.D.F.C.

My dearest Father,

May Jesus always assist you with His grace and make you holy.

I implore you, for the love of Jesus, to examine the report I am about to give you concerning my spirit carefully and not to be cursory and kind in wishing to judge me well. Since I know I can be a victim of deception, help me, with the grace of the heavenly Father, to escape such as soon as possible.

My ordinary way of praying is this: as soon as I begin to pray, I suddenly feel my soul beginning to recollect itself in a peace and tranquility hard to express in words. My senses remain suspended, with the exception of my hearing, which sometimes is not suspended, though this sense usually does not cause me trouble and I have to confess that even if there were a great deal of noise around me, it would not bother me in the least.

From this you will understand that few are the times when I manage to contemplate with my intellect.

Very often, what happens to me then is that when the continuous thought of God, of whom I am always aware, distances itself a bit from my mind, I suddenly feel myself touched by our Lord right at the center of my soul in a such a soothing and penetrating way that, more often than not, I am forced to shed tears of sorrow for my infidelity and for the tender mercy of having a Father who is so good to call me back to His presence.

At other times, instead, I find myself in great aridity and my body is greatly oppressed by its many infirmities. I feel that it is impossible to pull myself together to pray despite my good intentions and desires.

This state of affairs continues to become so intense that it will be a miracle of the Lord if I do not die from it. When it pleases the blessed Spouse of souls to bring an end to this torment, He suddenly sends me such spiritual devotion that it is irresistible. In an instant I find myself totally changed, enriched by supernatural graces, and so full of strength as to challenge the entire kingdom of Satan.

What I can say about this prayer is that my soul seems completely lost in God, and at such moments my soul progresses more than it possibly could in many years of very intense spiritual work.

Many other times I feel myself filled with such intense passion that I languish for God, and it truly seems to me that I will die. All of this does not come about from mental effort or reflection, but from an internal flame and a love that is so extreme that if God did not come to my aid quickly I would be consumed by it.

In the past I would sometimes manage with effort to calm this transport [of love], but now I am defenseless. Without fear of erring, I wish to say that I do not contribute to this in any way. At these moments I feel an intense, ardent desire to depart from this life, and, that desire not being satisfied, my soul suffers a most bitter and at the same time delightful pain so that it does not wish for it to cease.

It seems to my soul that everyone else finds consolation and relief in their ills and that it alone is in pain. The torment that keeps penetrating my soul to its very core is so much greater than its own weak nature that it would be impossible to suffer this were it not for the merciful Lord, who mitigates the violence with certain raptures, through which the poor fluttering thing becomes calm and quiet, both because the Lord gave the soul a foretaste of what it so desires and because of the high things He sometimes reveals to it.

A great desire to serve God with perfection also comes to me. Then it is no torment for my soul to suffer with cheerfulness. Even this happens without any reflection on my part, and quite suddenly. My soul does not understand where its great courage comes from.

These desires consume my soul internally because it understands, by the bright light God gives it, that it cannot give to God the service it desires. Then everything ends in the pleasures with which God comes to flood the soul.

It gives me great pain to deal with others, except those people with whom one speaks of God and of the preciousness of the soul. This is why I love solitude so much.

Very often I undergo great hardship to care for the necessities of life, that is, eating, drinking, and sleeping; and only because God wills it, I submit to these as one condemned.

It seems to me that time flies by rapidly and I never have enough for prayer. I am very fond of good literature, but I read very little both because I am hindered by my infirmities and because, after opening a book and reading briefly, I find myself so profoundly absorbed my reading becomes prayer.

Since the Lord has done these things, I feel myself totally changed. I no longer even recognize myself.

I clearly see that if there is any good at all in me, it comes from these supernatural gifts. Thus I acknowledge having reached a steadfast determination to suffer everything with submission and eagerness—though, alas, with so many imperfections—without tiring of suffering. My intensely firm resolution is to never offend God, not even venially; I would suffer death by fire a thousand times before deliberately committing any sin.

I feel so much improved through obedience to my confessor and the spiritual director of my soul that I would consider myself little less than damned were I to act contrary to them in anything.

If conversations are prolonged so as to pass the time, and I cannot politely leave, I have to force myself with immense effort to stay, because such conversations trouble me greatly.

I have never experienced anything supernatural that did not result in a notable benefit to myself. In addition to the individual effects, such heavenly favors produce three principal effects: an admirable knowledge of God and of His incomprehensible greatness; great self-knowledge and a profound sense of humility in recognizing my audacity in offending such a holy Father; and a great disdain for all earthly things as well as a great love for God and for the virtues.

Through these celestial treasures, I also acknowledge having reached a very great desire to deal with people who have made progress on the path to perfection. I love them very much because it seems to me that they assist me greatly in loving God, the Author of all these wonders. I am also strongly driven to abandon myself in everything to Divine Providence and nothing, favorable or unfavorable, worries me. All of this comes about without the least anxiety or concern.

In the past I experienced confusion at the thought that others would find out what the Lord was doing in me, but for some time now I no longer feel this confusion. I see that I am not better than others because of these favors. On the contrary, I see myself as worse, and that I make little progress despite all of these graces. This is how I view myself: I do not know if there are others worse than me. When I see things that seem to be sins in others, I cannot be convinced that they have offended God, even though I see it clearly. The only thing that concerns me is the common evil, which very often saddens me tremendously.

This is what ordinarily tries my soul. But sometimes, in fact rarely, it happens that for a period of time, perhaps even several days, these favors are removed. They are erased from my mind in such a way that I do not remember even the least good that had been in me. It seems that my spirit is completely surrounded by darkness and I cannot recall anything from before.

All my bodily and spiritual ills torment me. I feel troubled in spirit, and in this state I would like, I will not say pray because that would be too much, to form a single thought of God. But here everything becomes impossible for me. I see then that I am full of imperfections; all the courage I once felt in the past abandons me completely. I see myself very weak in the practice of virtue, in resisting the enemy's assaults. I am convinced then, more than ever, that I am good for nothing. I am assailed by profound sadness, and the terrible thought crosses my mind that I could be a delusional dreamer without even realizing it. God alone knows what a torment this is for me! Can it be—I think to myself—that in punishment for my infidelities the Lord allows me to deceive myself and my spiritual directors? If by the light I carry within my soul I know all too well the many failures into which I topple involuntarily, despite the many treasures the Lord has given to me, what can I do to conquer my doubt?

What I grasp with truth and clarity is that my heart loves, loves greatly, more than the intellect realizes. No doubt can assail this love, and I am so certain of loving that, except for the truths of faith, I am certain of nothing as much as this.

I can say with surety that I do not offend God more than usual even in this state because, thank heaven, I never lose my trust in Him. Everything passes with the first visit the Lord pays me. My intellect is filled with light; I feel my strength and all good desires revived, and even my bodily infirmities are much alleviated. I have carefully observed this more than once.

Judge for yourself, my dear father, if the demon's deceit exists in what I have revealed to you thus far, and open to me your inner thoughts in this regard, always as Jesus wills.

[FRA PIO]

"God wants to espouse the soul in faith."

In this letter to Father Agostino, Padre Pio appears a master of authentic spiritual life in his steady ascent on the rungs of the ladder of mystical union. In fact, he clearly explains all the steps necessary to reach union with God, which is a question of a "pure" union of faith. However, this union is celebrated through a process of purification from all actual and habitual imperfections, so that the creation wounded by sin, becomes a new creation [167].

Pietrelcina, December 19, 1913

∽

I.M.I.D.F.C.

My dearest Father,

May Jesus be with you always.

For the approaching blessed holiday of Christmas, with my heart on my lips and with more than filial affection, I send my most sincere wishes, as I make a promise to the little child Jesus for your spiritual and temporal happiness.

May the newborn Babe welcome my humble and feeble prayers, which I will raise up to Him with more lively faith in these holy days for you, for all the superiors, for the whole world!

May it also please this heavenly Infant to welcome my desires, which are to love Him as much as a creature can love Him here on earth and to see Him loved by all people in the same way!

Finally may He let some heavenly rays fall on the hearts of those afflicted souls! Presently, I do not have any advice to suggest to them, except to say that their fate is enviable. In seeing them so downcast, I rejoice in spirit and feel the holy envy of emulation. Their state, and above all the state of that particular one, dear father, is such that at the present time they are incapable of feeling comfort from whatever good word may be offered to them.

God has plunged their intellects into darkness, their wills in aridity, their memories in emptiness, their hearts in bitterness, dejection, and extreme despair. And all of this is greatly enviable because it all comes together in order to ready and prepare their hearts to receive the true form of the spirit, which is nothing other than the union of love.

God is with them, and this should be enough to convince them to be ever ready to dedicate their wills completely to God and to work in His service and for His honor. Let them not concern themselves at all with the fact that their will to dedicate themselves to God and to do all for the glory and honor of the divine Majesty once produced a particularly gentle and sweet effect in their spirit and sensory appetites. This was all mere fortuity. God grants such things to weak souls who are still infants in spirit, but removes these things from souls already fortified in spirit.

God wants to espouse the soul in faith, and the soul that is to celebrate this heavenly union must walk in pure faith, which is the only appropriate way to this union of love. In order to rise toward divine contemplation, I say that the soul must be purified of all actual imperfections and habitual imperfections, which consist of certain attachments and imperfect habits, which the purging of the senses did not succeed in eradicating—and which remain rooted in the soul—and one obtains with the purging of the spirit, by which God, with a most exalted light, penetrates all of the soul, pierces it intimately, and renews it completely.

This most exalted light, which God causes to descend into these souls, invests them in a demanding way and, laying waste their spirits, causes extreme afflictions and mortal interior pains to souls. Presently they are incapable of understanding this divine action, this most exalted light, for two reasons. In the first place, the light, which is so lofty and so sublime as to surpass the soul's ability to understand, is sooner a source of darkness and torment than of light. In the second place, this most exalted light is not only unintelligible but painful and distressful because of the soul's baseness and impurity. So, rather than consoling them, it makes them sorrowful, fills them with great pains of the sensory appetites, grave anxieties, and horrendous pain in their spiritual powers.

All of this happens at the beginning, when the divine light finds souls unprepared for the divine union. Therefore, it invests these souls in a purgative way; and when this light has purified them, it then invests them in an illuminative way, raising them up to the vision of and perfect union with God.

Therefore, let them rejoice in the Lord for raising them to this high place, and let them trust in the Lord fully as did holy Job, whom God placed in the same state and who hoped to see the light beyond the darkness.

Before closing, I would be curious to know why that soul does not draw near to the sacred table every day.

Please relay my best wishes to the whole community—and repay a hundred-fold Father Paolino's greetings—that they might pray for me as I do for them.

On the part of all our acquaintances accept their most sincere regards.

FRA PIO

❧ 17 ❧

"The true remedy is to lean on the cross of Jesus."

Padre Pio finally describes the flame that invades him with an intense love. As he recounts, it is a very delicate and gentle flame that does not cause pain. Confined in the realm of the ineffable, he cannot express how much the Divine Spouse increases the growth of his interior life. In this letter, Padre Pio illustrates his experience with a quaint story of a humble shepherd boy who, ushered into the private chambers of the King, simply cannot describe what he has seen to his fellow shepherds [183].

Pietrelcina, March 26, 1914

❧

J.M.J.D.F.C.

My dearest Father,

May our Lord always be in your heart and sanctify you.

Five months have already passed since I sent you the last report regarding my spirit.

Since that time the merciful Lord has helped me powerfully with His grace. The Lord God has bestowed very great gifts on my soul, and it seems to me that with such abundant aids, my spirit has been improving [as you will see] in what I am about to say. May all creatures give Him everlasting praise and blessings!

As soon as I begin to pray I feel my heart invaded by a flame of living love. This flame is unlike any flame of this poor world. It is a delicate and very gentle flame that consumes and gives no pain whatsoever. It is so sweet and delightful that the spirit finds great pleasure in it, and remains satiated by it in such a way as to not lose its desire for it. And, O God, it is a thing of such supreme wonder for me. Perhaps I shall never be able to understand it until I am in the heavenly country.

Far from removing the soul's sense of repletion, this desire refines it more and more. Rather than diminishing the desire, the enjoyment the soul feels at its core becomes more perfected. The same can be said of the desire to always enjoy this most lively flame, since the desire is not extinguished by enjoyment, but is further refined.

By this you will understand that the times are becoming rarer when I rely on intellectual reasoning, and more frequent are the times when I take advantage of my senses.

I do not know whether I have made myself understood, but I do not know how to explain myself any better. The soul that is placed in such a state by the Lord, enriched by such heavenly knowledge, should be more loquacious, and yet this is not the case. It has become almost mute. I do not know if this phenomenon has happened only to me. In very general terms, and, more often than not, terms that are emptied of any sense, the soul manages to express a small particle of what the Spouse is doing within.

Believe me, my father, all this is not an easy trial for the soul to bear. In this case, what happens is similar to what would happen if a poor shepherd boy were ushered into a royal chamber where a clutter of precious objects was gathered, the likes of which he had never seen. When he leaves the royal chamber, the shepherd will surely have all those objects, precious and beautiful, before his mind's eye though he cannot know their number nor be able to assign them their proper names. He might wish to speak with others about all that he has seen. He might gather all his intellectual and scientific powers to attempt this task, but realizing that all of his efforts would fail to make understood what he intends, he prefers to remain silent.

This is what usually happens to my soul, which divine Goodness alone has elevated to this level of prayer. But alas, my father, I know that strictly speaking this comparison does not hold.

All of these extraordinary things, far from being stopped, become more elevated. I feel that the raptures have increased in strength and usually come with such a driving force that any efforts to impede them are worthless. The Lord has given my soul greater detachment from the things of this poor world, and I feel He continues reinforcing this always more with a blessed freedom of spirit.

It seems to me that God has poured many graces into the depths of my soul with regards to compassion for the miseries of others, especially the poor. The great compassion my soul feels at the sight of a needy person gives birth, at its very core, to a most intense desire to succor him and, if I heeded my will, I would be compelled to take off my own garments to clothe him.

If I know that a person is afflicted, whether in body or in soul, what I would not do for the Lord to see that person freed from his ailments? For his salvation I would willingly take on all his afflictions, if the Lord permitted, I would give up the fruits of these sufferings for him.

I see very well that this is a most particular favor from God. Though in the past I never failed, by divine mercy, to help the needy, by nature I had if no pity at all then only a little for their miseries.

Thanks to the favors God has not ceased to heap upon me, I have improved a great deal in my trust in God. If in the past it sometimes seemed to me that I needed the help of others, I now no longer do. Through my own experience I know that the true remedy for not falling is to lean on the cross of Jesus, trusting in Him alone who, for our salvation, chose to be hung on it.

I have and I continue to pray for all those intentions that you desire, but I refrain from asking the Lord for a response, since He forbade me to do so. If in the past the Lord permitted, or rather, wished to be asked what His will was in this or that circumstance, He has reproved this old way of acting for some time now. Our Lord once said to me, "This way is well suited for those who are like infants on my path, and I wish for you to finally leave that infancy."

I implore you, pray for him who intercedes on your behalf with very weak but continuous prayers to our Lord.

Your son,

FRA PIO

The Lord will repay you for the applications you sent.

❧ *18* ❧

"No one is spotless before the Lord."

Realism is an unmistakable trait of mystics. When Padre Pio wrote, he did not consider himself holy, rather, as one barely touched by the holiness of God, and this only to illuminate the misery of his sins. Padre Pio is aware that his youth was marked by guilt (Ps 24:7), but the severity of God toward sin is balanced by the gentleness of God's mercy [191].

Pietrelcina, May 27, 1914

❧

I.M.I.D.F.C.

My dearest Father,

May Jesus and Mary be always in your heart and make you holy.

I received together with your letter, the letter from that soul. I am thankful for the Lord's pity, for in my abjectness He does not deprive me of your welcome correspondence, of which I acknowledge myself unworthy.

I read that person's letter, which you sent with yours, and, that person permitted me to respond directly, as this was the

Lord's will.[29] I hope that I have not merited your censure for not following your suggestion. If the liberty I took has caused you the least inconvenience, I immediately declare that I withdraw it and promise to never again take such liberties in the future. But I did not believe I was doing any harm, and I did not act according to my own will.

At this moment, my father, my spirit is severely oppressed. It seems to me that my life has come to a halt. My heart is shattered by a most acute sorrow that fills me completely. A dense darkness thickens on the horizon of my spirit, which only the mercy of the One who authors it can and must dispel.

In the meanwhile, my soul decays under the weight of its infidelities toward the Author of life. I know that no one is spotless before the Lord, but my impurity is limitless before Him. In my present state the merciful Lord, in His infinite wisdom and justice, deigns to raise the veil and reveal my hidden shortcomings in all their malignancy and ugliness, and I see myself so deformed that my very clothing shrinks in horror from my defilement. This grim portrait is not painted by a man, with whom the soul could easily exculpate itself, but by God, who, for a little while, acts as a Judge with whom there is no appeal.

---

29. In this letter Padre Pio makes reference to persons who have either written to him directly—as is the case here—or who have been referred to him by his own spiritual director (cf. the postscript). Padre Pio refers to these people as *anima* ("soul"), or *persona* ("person"). The gender of the individuals mentioned is unclear since, in the Italian, both of *anima* and *persona* as well as their respective pronouns are feminine.

In this state no creature, whether human or angelic, no matter how worthy, can stand between the poor soul and God the Judge, who reveals so grim a portrait.

O for those happy days of my life when my most gentle Good was with me and lived inside my heart! Where have you gone? Living is difficult for me, O God, and in the bitterness of my heart the road is clear to lamentation! Do not recall here, O most clement Father, the faults of my youth[30] now that you have forgotten them! Alas, my God, let me weep over my sins. It would have been better for me if no human eye had seen me, if I would have perished inside the womb.[31]

These are the lamentations of my soul in this state. Now what must I do? I submit myself with resignation to this action of the divine Doctor, knowing from long experience that all will end with the triumph of God's glory and the soul's benefit.

In the meantime, may it please the Lord in His goodness to quickly veil His great majesty, which acts as judge of my soul, so that I will not remain crushed and terrified. May He give me words to defend my cause before Him and strength to endure His gaze.

Alas, my father, what will become of us when we appear with all our deeds before this God, our Judge! If we suffer such terror now when He simply lifts the veil that hides our faults from our eyes so that we might look upon them in their deformity, what will happen when we appear before Him to endure the severity of His gaze!

---

30. Cf. Ps 25:7.

31. Cf. Job 10:18.

O God, if everyone knew that Your severity is equal to Your gentleness, what creature would be so foolish as to dare to offend You?

My God, three times just and three times holy, show Your severe justice to all who dare to offend You, so that they will learn if not to love than at least to fear You.

When will I have the comfort of embracing you again, my father?

Bless me and pray to Jesus for me.

FRA PIO

You can assure that soul you referred to in your letter before last to remain calm and not to fear, as that person has no reason to fear; the person's soul is most acceptable to the Lord. I thank the person for his prayers for me, and I would entreat him, through you, not to cease praying. Only God knows how much I, too, pray for his perfection.

⟨ *19* ⟩

"I pray incessantly to the divine Infant on everyone's behalf."

It was a few days before Christmas 1914, and the world stood on the brink of World War I, when Padre Pio, whose precarious health still obliged him to live with his family in Pietrelcina, wrote to Father Agostino of his fear of being cut off from the Capuchins. Yet, he perceives that he is enveloped in the faith of daily fulfilling the will of God [220].

Pietrelcina, December 19, 1914

⟨

I.M.I.D.F.C.

My dearest father,

May the grace of the heavenly Father be with you always and make you ever more worthy of the country of blessed districts. So be it.

I am writing these few lines from my bed so that the holy day of Baby Jesus' birth might not pass without my wishing them to be full of the most select graces for you.

I believe it is unnecessary to reassure you that I pray incessantly to the divine Infant on everyone's behalf, and especially for you. It would be a outrage not to do so, for many are the bonds that unite me to you.

During this time, in addition to laying my humble prayers for you at the feet of Baby Jesus, I will again spread my tears and offer up all the bitterness that oppresses my heart.

What a humiliation for me, my father, to see myself practically cut off from the Franciscan Order! Despite my readiness, I was overcome with acute sorrow as soon as father provincial's letter arrived communicating his decisions.[32]

The tears I shed were so many and caused such harm to my well-being that I was forced to take to my bed, where I still find myself. May God's divine will be done. Perhaps a bit of solace will be granted to me during these holy feast days?! I am ready for anything!

I wrote Father Paolino right away and only in obedience to you; I let him know the will of God regarding that business.[33] I hope for its success.

I thought it better to write to him first, waiting, for the time-being to write to that soul. As soon as I have an answer from Paolino, God willing, I will write to that soul.

If Father Paolino does not bend in the matter I have communicated to him, please do tell me whether or not I should stop writing to that poor woman to communicate to her heaven's will.

---

32. Padre Pio's illness made it physically impossible for him to remain in any of the Order's monasteries, since merely being in a monastery seemed to trigger his acute symptoms. When his superiors insisted that he return to the community, Pio asked for a "brief," a document which would allow him to live as a Capuchin friar outside the monastery. Despite the superior's personal reservations, he acquiesced and obtained Padre Pio's brief.

33. Padre Pio had written to Father Paolino on December 15 on the subject of correspondence between a director and the soul being directed.

Pray for this very unhappy son of yours.

FRA PIO, CAPUCHIN

Can we eat meat on Christmas Day? I beg for your speedy response.

·◇· *20* ·◇·

"I am crucified by love!
I simply cannot endure this any longer."

This particularly meaningful letter in Padre Pio's journey narrates the appearance of the stigmata. Padre Pio's testimony is reminiscent of the psalmist who speaks of specific parts of the body (Ps 106:18) in reference to the soul where desires, aspirations, and longing abide. The holy man describes the Lord as kissing and touching his soul [235].

Pietrelcina, March 18, 1915

·◇·

J.M.J.D.F.C.

My dearest father,

May Jesus and Mary be with you always and with all of those by whom they are sincerely loved. So be it.

I am answering your most precious letter after two long days of delay because the crisis, of which I have referred to elsewhere, has become accentuated more than ever in these days. At present, I can barely manage to jot on paper these brief words.

Father, grant that I may unburden myself at least to you: I am crucified by love! I simply cannot endure this any longer. This fare is very delicate for one accustomed to much coarser foods, and this is exactly what continually produces such strong spiritual indigestion within me, to the point that my poor soul groans in the most animated pain and love. The poor little thing does not know how to adapt to this new way of being treated by the Lord. The kiss and, I would say, significant touch the most loving, heavenly Father impresses on my soul still produces extreme pain.

May the good Jesus help you to understand my true state! Meanwhile, I entreat you to continue using a little more charity with me and making yourself clear in this regard.

My dearest father, satisfying life's necessities: eating, drinking, sleeping, etc., weighs heavily on me and I am hard pressed to find an analogy to describe it if not the pains the martyrs experienced during their ultimate trials. Father, do not think that this simile is an exaggeration; no, it is exactly like that. If the Lord, in His goodness, does not remove as in the past [the gift of] reflection from me while I satisfy such needs, I feel I will not be able to endure this long. I feel the earth eroding beneath my feet. May the Lord help and liberate me from so much anguish! Let Him treat me as I deserve. I am a constant rebel against divine action and do not deserve to be treated in this way at all.

Accept, O father, my most sincere wishes, which I send with my whole heart, for your name day. Let the good God hear all the wishes I offer on your behalf. May God grant you a dazzling sunset, much more splendid than the dawn of your life. This is my most beautiful wish for you.

The good Jesus wants to console that soul through me with direct correspondence. To act differently would increase the poor woman's confusion and maker her burden greater. To this end, and to avoid possible and serious difficulties, we could address my letters intended for her to her confessor.

I beg you—should you find it just—to send me her confessor's address. I realize that this appears extremely confusing, but we cannot act otherwise. You already know how intransigent God is about certain things.

I cannot go on. I end by asking for your paternal blessing and a prayer to the Lord on my behalf, for my sincere conversion.

Your humble,

FRA PIO, CAPUCHIN

❧ *21* ❧

"My crisis is extremely painful."

Composed and dated on the same day as the previous letter, this letter confirms Padre Pio's need for corresponding during his stay in Pietrelcina, symbolic of his desire to communicate with his spiritual director in a timely manner. It is understandable that being far from the one person who illuminated him in wisdom, he wished to see him again or, at least, to receive some letters in response to his own [236].

Pietrelcina, March 18, 1915

❧

I.M.I.D.F.C.

My dearest Father,

May the Spirit make you holy and illuminate you further concerning eternal goods, reserved for us by the goodness of the heavenly Father. So be it.

May Jesus give you knowledge of my current state. I am crucified by love, my dear father! My crisis is extremely painful.

Pray to Jesus for me and do not fail to write lengthy and frequent letters to me, having pity on me if you do not receive a response.

I would like to see you again, and, to tell the truth, I was expecting as much while you were on your way back from your mission. Jesus did not wish it, may He be blessed ever more!

I cannot continue; my present state of mind does not allow me. Have pity on me.

I bid you good-bye in the holy kiss of the Lord.

Bless me always.

FRA PIO, CAPUCHIN

❧ 22 ❧

"Jesus said to me..."

In this message, Padre Pio prophesies Italy's entrance into World War I. He also confesses to feeling compelled to intercede on behalf of people he does not even know, and he observes with wonder how Jesus heeds his prayers for this precise group of people, evidently in need of sound help [249].

Pietrelcina, April 21, 1915

❧

J.M.J.D.F.C.

My dearest Father,

May the flames of divine love consume in you all that is not pleasing to the eyes of the divine Spouse. May Jesus make you holy. So be it.

Jesus came this morning and, having asked Him how I was supposed to answer your questions, He said to me, "In compensation for the toil he endured for My glory, your father has been granted happiness of spirit.... Several means have been undertaken to make the spirit of the Founder [St. Francis] bloom again in the province; the fruits of these means are still few. Have him persevere and keep watch so that the means undertaken are not forgotten too quickly."[34]

Jesus stopped here for a while and shortly thereafter continued, "Italy, my child, did not wish to listen to the voice of love. Know, however, that for some time I have been holding back the arm of My Father, who wants to cast His thunderbolts upon His adulterous daughter. We were hoping that the misfortunes of others would have made her examine herself, would have caused her to intone the *miserere* at the right moment. She did not appreciate even this last trace of My love, and it is for this reason that her sin has become more abominable before me... The same fate that has befallen her siblings is certainly hers as well."

Father, do become angry if perhaps I leave some of your questions unanswered—I do not know [the answer to] one and am unaware of the other. But have no doubt; if it pleases God to tell me something in that regard, I promise I will refer it to you right away, knowing full well that my duty persists to answer your questions.

How is it, O father, that when I am with Jesus everything I intend and wish to ask Him is not called to mind? Yet, I feel an acute sorrow for this forgetfulness. How can it be explained? No one's explanation has been able to fully convince me up to now.

Listen, then, to a much stranger thing. Even when I am with Jesus, I ask Him things I never had in mind to ask, to intercede for those for whom I never intended to pray and, what

---

34. One and half lines of text are crossed out in the original letter in such a way as to make it impossible to transcribe them.

is more wonderful, at times for those whom I have never known, seen, or heard of. And here it must be noted that when this happens, I have never known Jesus to refuse what I ask on behalf of these people.

I give animated thanks to Jesus for the assurances that, in His name, you sent in your last letter. I pray then that, in showing me the charity of writing, you would add the additional charity of writing very lengthy letters.

I realize that I am being very presumptuous with you, but pity my weakness. In my present state, your letters give me a tiny bit of light.

FRA PIO

23

"I know very well that the cross is a token of love."

The answers Father Agostino offers to Padre Pio's frequent questions shed "light from Paradise," and are "beneficial dew" during his demanding spiritual and mystical journey while still forced to stay with his family. Facing his own vulnerability and emotional excitability, Pio blushes at his temperament that demands consolation [250].

Pietrelcina, April 21, 1915

·❧·

I.M.I.D.F.C.

My dearest Father,

May Jesus make you holy and grant you all the good that you desire for the souls of others. So be it.

Long live Jesus! Your last letter brought a bit of consolation to my extremely embittered spirit. With this letter you shed a bit of light on my spirit. Though a very tenuous light, thank heaven it is enough to be able to see where to place my feet so as not to trip; it is a light that communicates to me the strength to drag my cross and to feel that its enormous weight is less heavy.

My face blushes. I know very well that the cross is a token of love, a pledge of pardon, and that a love not fed and nurtured by the cross is not true love, but rather is reduced to a fire of straw. Yet, even with this knowledge, this false disciple of the Nazarene feels the cross weighing heavily on his heart, and many times (do not be scandalized and horrified, O father, by what I am about to say) he goes in search of a merciful Cyrene to relieve and comfort him.

What worth can my love possibly have before God? I fear greatly that my love for God may not be a true love. This is also one of the swords among many others, which oppress me at moments, and I feel myself at the point of being crushed.

Yet, my father, I have a very great desire to suffer for the love of Jesus. But how is it that when I am faced with trials, contrary to my will, I seek some solace? How much strength and violence I must muster up within me during these trials so as to reduce to silence my temperament, let's call it that, which demands consolation.

I do not want to feel this struggle. Many times it makes me weep like a child because it seems that it comes from a lack of love and conformity to God. What do you have to say about this?

Write to me, when Jesus wills it, and always at length. I await your answers to my many problems, doubts, and difficulties as light from Paradise, as a beneficial dew on a thirsty plant.

Bless me, O father, and always pray for he who continually remembers you before the Lord.

The archpriest, my family, and friends all send their regards and cordially salute you.

Your poor, humble son,

FRA PIO, CAPUCHIN

24

"I know not what all of this means for me."

In this letter, Padre Pio expresses urgency for the guidance of Father Benedetto, his former spiritual director. Padre Pio asked Father Agostino to read all of his letters to Father Benedetto, in order to receive from the latter a "life or death sentence," meaning his sanction to continue along the already undertaken road to spiritual wisdom or to abandon it [280].

Pietrelcina, September 4, 1915

❧·

J.M.J.D.F.C.

My dearest Father,

May Jesus always be the supreme King of your heart. So be it.

To find out from father lector that your not having replied or answered certain doubts that crossed my soul, to find out that you remained deaf and indifferent to my Calvary not because you wished me to experience your silence, but rather because of your innocent forgetfulness, revives me slightly and is a sweet comfort in the midst of so much bleakness of spirit to which the Lord wishes to subject his poor servant.

My present state, both physical and moral, is very desolate and it is absolutely impossible, even in the smallest way, to describe it to you. From the letters I wrote to Father Agostino you can form a more or less adequate idea of the state that I have once more been in for some time now. I do not know what this all means for me. I do not know if I am worthy of hatred or of love.

I beg you, therefore, to read the letters father lector gives you, and then to pass your judgment on the matter. Please, my father, do not refuse me an answer simply because you may have to pronounce a judgment that may appear discouraging to me.

Relieve me, for the love of the Sorrowful Virgin Mother, from such a cruel uncertainty. Save me if I have drowned. Raise me up again if you see that I have fallen.

As I await your life or death sentence, I wish you every heavenly consolation from the most gentle Jesus, and, kissing your hand, I beg you to consider this most unworthy son of yours worthy of your paternal blessing

FRA PIO, CAPUCHIN

BOOK II

VICTIM TO CONSOLE THE HEART OF JESUS

Preface

"It is no longer I who live..." (Gal 2:20)

The Stigmatic Priest

The heart of Christian existence is the discovery that Jesus Christ is both he who is called and he who calls. In as much as he is the Mediator between God and humanity (cf. Acts 17:31), Christ is called by the Father, but it is from Christ that mediation descends. In the history of Christianity, the Christian intercedes in as much as he or she is called, upon conversion, to live in the Church, to be an evangelizer, and, for some, a priest. The priest's intercession unifies the contemplative charism—one individual for the many, one individual for the community, one individual in whom the community recognizes itself and comes together. Gathered here are Padre Pio's letters which indicate that being a priest and having the gift of the stigmata are inseparably joined in his person.

If the prophetic charism must remain in the Church until the final coming of the glorious Lord, and if the stigmata are part of the permanence of this charism even in the current history of the Church, then Padre Pio will surely be remembered for having been the *first* stigmatic priest. In the dialectic of word and sign characteristic of Christian revelation, there must certainly be present here, in a hidden way, a meaning valid for all priests and for all those who, with faith and love, are on their way to becoming priests. In fact, in the saintly Capuchin, Pio from Pietrelcina, the mark of the stigmata cannot be understood correctly apart from his priesthood. The characteristics of a priestly spirituality, which in this perspective can be inferred from these letters, hold not only the classic canons of Christian mysticism, but also the characteristic of an unmistakable relevance to the present day.

The selection of letters in this second volume contain the theme of the stigmatization, and can be grouped under the following three themes: the description of the happiness experienced by the soul in meeting God, revealed particularly in his Son, Jesus; references to the soul's suffering; texts that express the desire to fulfill the will of the heavenly Father. These are also the means by which Padre Pio, *as a priest* marked by the stigmata, lived his consecration for the spread of the kingdom of God and the good of all souls. These means channel every priestly existence, the young and not so young, to Christ the Priest.

The King's Secret Must Not Be Revealed

With the mark and gift of the stigmata, Padre Pio was a priest who possessed a secret that could not be revealed, the secret of every priestly existence: the King who is the Father of Jesus Christ. Padre Pio's life is an unequivocal demonstration of the deeply personal relationship that exists between God and the consecrated person who works and announces *in persona Christi*. It is a relationship that Padre Pio expressed by citing the Song of Songs (6:3): "I am my beloved's and my beloved is mine."

It is interesting to note that among the books of the Old Testament most quoted in Padre Pio's letters are Job, the Psalms, and the Song of Songs. The first two appear above all in the letters written during Padre Pio's dark night to describe his spiritual suffering, his identification with the sinner who perceives himself as distant from God, and his identification with Job who, assailed by suffering, sought a stable reference in God. But the love for and joy found in the Beloved that the holy man of Gargano experiences are especially revealed in his use of the words from the Song of Songs, "Tell him that until a soul has come to receive this kiss, it can never seal a covenant with him" (cf. Song 1:2). Padre Pio lives the strong tension of this love, he seeks it, he possesses it, and he desires it anew. Jesus is no longer merely a model, but such a captivating presence that Padre Pio desires to make his own the words of St. Paul: "It is no longer I who live, but it is Christ who lives in me" (Gal 2:20).

Padre Pio's desire for Jesus' presence becomes a true assimilation of the Son of God in his life and produces a profound sweetness. In the early letters (1910–1912), we perceive the complete joy this priestly and stigmatic soul feels in being inhabited by Christ: "It is my happiness that the Lord allows me to savor almost only in afflictions." What the Lord accomplishes in Padre Pio's soul is the result of a true seduction, which compels him to offer himself to *console* Jesus, and, through his contact with Christ, introduces him to an atmosphere of profound serenity. In fact, in a letter dated August 10, 1911, written on the occasion of his priestly ordination, Padre Pio expresses himself thus: "I keep comparing the peace I felt in my heart on that day with the peace I began to feel the evening before, and I find no difference." The letters of this period, which obviously precede the stigmatization, are rich with similar phrases. There shines forth the fact that Padre Pio knew Jesus as a person with whom he enjoyed a completely gratifying, captivating, and, above all, reassuring personal relationship—characteristics that are an enduring foundation in a priest's life. Padre Pio understands the authentic value of Christ, and he is ready to pay any price for that field wherein he has found this hidden treasure (cf. Mt 13:44).

The Suffering of the Soul

The holy man from Gargano often uses the Psalms to praise the Lord, and the book of Job as an example of patience. These two books, as well as quotes from the book of Jonah, serve to describe the suffering that Padre Pio experiences during his "dark night," prior to and immediately after the gift of the stigmata. What is the meaning of that mystical phenomenon called the "dark night"? As described by Padre Pio in his letters, the "dark night" can be traced back to spiritual experiences of profound serenity and sweetness that a soul experienced in its personal relationship with God (Letter 5).

In order to ascend to divine union with the Bridegroom, it is necessary for the soul to be purified of every imperfection. This purification comes about through what Padre Pio calls "a most exalted light." This light invests the soul in a "demanding" way, causing it "extreme afflictions and mortal interior pains." What is most bewildering during this period is that the soul cannot understand God's action in it, and, therefore, it is overcome with great anguish and suffering. The very thought of this oppresses the soul to the point that only by God's special grace is it prevented from going astray. And this grace unites within Padre Pio a feeling of profound sweetness and serenity in being permanently bound to the person of Jesus Christ, and in the dark night that generates a sense of privation and suffering.

For Padre Pio, clearly a son of Franciscan spirituality, Jesus is, before all else, Supreme Goodness. But this Supreme Goodness is quite different from the One who once filled his soul

with happiness during the initial stages of mystical life. While God reveals himself as complete Goodness, Padre Pio bitterly discovers that not only has God grown distant and, in doing so, left a tremendous void, but God does not allow himself to be found. It is from this perspective that Padre Pio writes his most heartfelt letters that express a profound sorrow that first reaches out to God and then to his spiritual director, from whom he invokes some light: "Can this sinful soul possibly be saved?" Evidently, the purifying moment is attained in absolute darkness when God is hidden and silent. For Padre Pio this moment is the passion, symbolized in the cry, "My God, my God, why have you forsaken me" (cf. Mt 27:46), a question he often poses to his spiritual director.

Jesus Is the Promised Land

As sign of the permanence of prophecy in the Church, Padre Pio's gift of the stigmata offers the holy man the awareness that he bears the weight of fidelity to the Word of God. And he can neither dispose of nor liberate himself from this burden because obedience in doing the will of the Father corresponds to fidelity to the Word received, apart from any external provocation or desire of people. The call to become a prophet possesses a character so bound to the Word that no person and no thing can detract from the fulfillment of this mission: *fiat voluntas tua*. Padre Pio knows very well that this means running along unknown paths and at times in clear opposition to human logic. It was not easy for him to remain faithful to the Word. His temptation to assent to people's wishes is glimpsed in several letters. The tension of having to choose between obedience to God and what people wanted to hear was not foreign to Padre Pio's spiritual life. On the contrary, he found that the choice between living a tranquil life with others and undergoing their chastisements for his fidelity was unavoidable.

The possibility of realizing this fidelity centers on the primary source of Padre Pio's mystical life: resembling Christ, the model of priestly life always more. In fact, for Padre Pio this progressive resemblance to the Word occurs in two moments: on the one hand it is Jesus who renders the person similar to himself, and on the other, it is Jesus who seeks to inhabit the person, to make his or her soul and senses truly and completely his own. In the case of Padre Pio, we find ourselves before a transforming union that is accompanied by mystical phenomena, among them fainting, torpor of strength and the senses, Love's wounds to the heart, the touch of God, and transverberation—all of which are a prelude to the stigmatization.

Most of the time Padre Pio seems to simply allow himself be carried by the greatness of these events. Thus, from the phenomenon of distance from God he passes into moments of extraordinary intimacy. Evagrio Pontico († 399), in his *De Oratione,* explains that in such experiences one is before an "infinite ignorance" of one's surroundings, to the point of going beyond ecstasy to a "catastacy," that is, an experience uniquely directed toward the vision and contemplation of God. Gregory of Nyssa (335–395) notes that this stage of light is followed by clouds and darkness, where the intellect is placed before its inability to contemplate God without having to go outside itself. At times Padre Pio speaks of God as hiding "behind a cloud" or in a "thick fog." At other times he is bursting with expressions of joy.

While love and sorrow are imprinted in his soul in an alternating of thick hazes and extraordinary flashes of light, Padre Pio enters into contact with the Absolute. Physical forces no longer resist and the Word becomes silence. The blessed Capuchin wrote in one of his more significant letters:

> I felt only once, in the most secret and intimate part of my spirit, something so delicate I do not know how to describe it. At first the soul felt His presence without seeing it, and then, I would say, He drew so near the soul that it felt His touch fully, just as when one body touches another to give you a pale comparison. I do not know what else to say except to confess that I was overcome by the greatest fright at first, and shortly afterward this fright was changed to a heavenly ecstasy. It seemed to me that I was no longer an exile and I cannot say whether I was aware of still being in my body when this happened. Only God knows, and I just do not know what to say to make you understand this event (Letter 4).

The culmination of Christ's work in the soul is the moment when it is intensely enveloped in a state of absolute peace and can fully accomplish the will of the Father, faithfully obeying the Word received. If this was true for Padre Pio, it is equally true for every priest, called to the same mission. The Divine Master is no longer simply Light, and Guide. He is the place wherein one realizes complete happiness. Jesus is the Promised Land where God manifests himself. Jesus is the milieu in which the Father reveals himself in the Spirit. Jesus is the living, revealing Word of the Father, who wrote in Padre Pio's life with the mark of the stigmata and suffering, thus confirming him as a true imitator of Francis of Assisi, and, like Francis, a true imitator of Christ.

GIANLUIGI PASQUALE, O.F.M. CAP.

⟡ *1* ⟡

"My God! Can all you point out to me possibly be true?"

At Father Agostino's request, Padre Pio unveils three great secrets. The first has to do with celestial visions, which began not long after his novitiate (1904) when Fra Pio was little more than 17 years old and had only begun to wear the Franciscan habit! The second secret is a confirmation that as a young man he had indeed already received the stigmata and its accompanying pain. However, the young monk immediately asked the Lord to free him from the phenomena. His prayer was granted, but the pain remained. The third secret concerns the often overlooked fact that Fra Pio also experienced the crowning with thorns and flagellation [290].

Pietrelcina, October 10, 1915

⟡

I.M.I.D.F.C.

My dearest father,

May the peace of Jesus guard your heart from every stain of guilt and may the most Blessed Virgin obtain for you, through her Son, the abundance of grace which makes you always walk, with complete humility and docility, in a manner worthy of your vocation. So be it.

I received your latest letter. I read it with stupor and I felt like I was daydreaming. My God! Can all that you point out to me possibly be true? Is it possible that the Lord is to be glorified in such an insignificant creature?

May the Lord be pleased to grant our common vows and make your dream for me come true! As for me, I will not stop weeping throughout the remaining hours of my life, for you know how my heart breaks to see so many blind unfortunates shunning, more than they would, fire the Divine Master-Teacher's sweetest invitation: "Come to me, all you who thirst and I will give you to drink" (cf. Jn 7:37).

My heart is extremely tormented when faced with such truly blind people, who feel no mercy whatsoever for themselves, their passions having stripped them of their judgment to the extent that they would never dream of going to drink from that true water of Paradise.

One glance, O father, and then tell me if I do not have reason for feeling unhappy because of the folly of these blind people. See how the enemies of the cross triumph more every day. O heavens! They continually burn in a living fire amid their thousand desires for earthly gratifications.

Jesus invites them to quench their thirst with his ever-living water. Jesus knows all too well how much they need to drink their fill of the new water he has prepared for those who truly thirst, so that they will not perish in the devouring flames.

To them Jesus extends His most tender invitation, "Come to me all you who thirst and I will give you to drink." But, my God, what do these unfortunates reply? They act as if they did not understand You, they flee from You, and, worse still, so accustomed are they by their many years of living in the fire of earthly gratifications and having grown old in those flames, these poor ones no longer hear your loving invitations and no longer even perceive the great, horrible danger they are in.

What remedy can one use to help these unhappy Judases to return to their senses? What remedy can one hope for so that they, who are truly dead, can come back to life? Ah, my father, my soul is bursting with sorrow! Jesus gave a greeting, an embrace, a kiss even to these souls; but for these miserable ones it was a greeting that did not sanctify, an embrace that did not convert, a kiss that alas, I was about to say did not save, but perhaps in the great majority of these cases will never save them!

Divine Mercy does not soften them any longer. They are neither drawn by benefits nor controlled by chastisements. With the gentle they are insolent, with the austere they rage, in prosperity they grow angry, in adversity they despair. Deaf, blind, unfeeling toward Divine Mercy's ever sweeter invitations and ever more terrible reproaches, which should rouse and convert them, they only grow hardened in their resolve and intensify their darkness.

But alas! O my father, how foolish I am! Who can assure me that I, too, am not among these unhappy souls? It is true that I thirst for the true water of Paradise, but who knows if it is really *that* water for which my soul desires so ardently?

And this torment becomes more intense to the extent that this water does not quench my thirst but, on the contrary, makes it even greater.

O father, is this not a compelling reason to strongly doubt that the water my poor soul desires is not the water our sweetest Savior invites us to drink of in great draughts?

May it please the Lord, Fountain of all life, not to deny me this sweet and precious water that He, in the eagerness of His love for humanity, promised to those who thirst. I yearn for this water, O my father, and with continuous groans and sighs I beseech Jesus for it. Do pray that it does not hide from me. O father, tell Jesus how great is my need for this water, which alone can heal a soul wounded by love.

May this most tender Bridegroom of the sacred song[1] console this soul who thirsts for Him; may He console this soul with that same divine kiss asked for by the holy bride. Tell Him that until the soul receives this kiss it will never be able to seal this covenant with Him: "I am everything for my beloved and my beloved is everything for me."[2]

May it please the Lord not to forsake those who have placed all their faith in Him. Alas! May my hope never flounder, and may I remain faithful to Him always....

In your resolute will to know, or rather, to receive an answer to your questions, I cannot fail to recognize the express will of God. So, with trembling hand and a heart overflowing with sorrow, unaware of the true cause, I prepare to obey you.

In your first question, you want to know when Jesus began to favor His poor creature with celestial visions. If I am not mistaken, they must have begun not long after my novitiate.[3]

Your second question is whether He has granted him[4] the ineffable gift of His holy stigmata. To this I must answer in the affirmative. The first time Jesus willed to permit him this favor they were visible, especially in one hand, and, since this soul was rather alarmed by such a phenomenon, it prayed the Lord to

---

1. The Old Testament book of the Song of Songs.

2. Song 6:23.

3. Padre Pio made his novitiate from January 1903 to January 1904.

4. At times, Padre Pio's sense of humility at the powerful work of God in his life causes him to refer to himself in the third person, or simply as "this soul" or "the soul."

withdraw such a visible sign. Thenceforth, they no longer appeared; however, though the wounds disappeared, the very acute pain that is felt along with the wounds did not, especially under some circumstances and on certain days.

Your third and last of question is whether, and how many times, the Lord has made this soul endure His crowning of thorns and flagellation. The response to this question must also be affirmative. As far as the number of times is concerned, I would not know how to determine this. All that I can say is that for many years this soul has suffered these almost once a week.

It seems to me that I have obeyed you. Is this not so?

Donna Raffaelina and her sister have not yet returned to their homeland. Pray diligently for both of these most-afflicted souls, especially for Raffaelina, who, more than her counterpart, needs divine help.

In another letter I have a surprise for you concerning Raffaelina. Meanwhile, pray so that everything prevails according to God's heart.

Respectfully, I kiss your hand; please deign to forever bless this son of yours.

FRA PIO

∿ 2 ∿

"Inexpressible sweetness rains from your eyes"

In this lengthy letter, Padre Pio's language, in a classic and biblical style, flows with the juxtaposition of opposites. In this way, he responds to five questions in the letter. He also writes that "his heart" either rejoices in the Lord or is tormented for Him, meaning that his entire person is affected (cf. 1 Sam 2:1) [292].

Pietrelcina, October 17, 1915

∿

I.M.I.D.F.C.

My dearest father,

May Jesus continue to keep His paternal gaze turned upon you; may He sustain you always with His grace and help you to fight the good fight, giving you a share of the reward that is given to strong souls. So be it.

How great, O father, is my misfortune! Who could possibly comprehend it? I know very well that I am a mystery to myself; I do not know how to understand myself.

You tell me that the venerable Sister Teresa used to say: "I do not wish to choose to live or to die; but may Jesus do what he will with me!" I see very well a similarity in all souls stripped of self and filled by God. Unfortunately, how far my soul is from being divested of self in this way! I cannot seem to check the urges of my heart, and yet I try so hard, O father, to conform to the venerable Sister Teresa's words, that must still be kindled in every soul by the love of God. But, to my mortification, I must confess I cannot seem to rise to this when I must remain a prisoner in a body of death. This is a sign that there is no love of God in me. Since there is but one Spirit that gives life, there should be but one effect. If what is at work in me is the same as that which was at work in Sister Teresa, that blessed soul's words would be realized in me as well. Now tell me, am I not right to doubt myself? Dear me! Who will free me of such harsh afflictions of my heart?

Dear God, I accept all the torments of the earth gathered into a bundle; I desire my share of them, but I cannot resign myself to being separated from You through a lack of love. Alas! For pity's sake, do not permit my poor soul to wander; do not allow my hope to fail. Let me never be separated from You, and if I am unaware of being already so separated, draw me back to You this instant. Comfort my intellect, dear God, that I may know myself well and the great love You have shown me, so that I may eternally enjoy the supreme beauty of Your divine countenance.

O dear Jesus, never let me lose so precious a treasure as You are for me. My Lord and my God, so alive in my soul is the ineffable sweetness that flows from Your eyes and the loving gaze which You, my Good, deign to cast upon this poor wretch.

How can the torment of my heart be calmed knowing it is far from You? My soul knows only too well the terrible battles I fought when You, my Beloved, hid Yourself from me! How vivid, O my sweet Lover, that terrible and thunderous image imprinted in this soul!

Who will ever separate or extinguish the fire that burns for You in my breast with such bright flames! Alas! O Lord, do not take pleasure in hiding Yourself from me. You know what confusion and anxiety take possession of all the soul's powers and sentiments! You see that this poor thing cannot stand under the cruel torment of abandonment because You let it fall so deeply in love with You, O infinite Beauty!

Indeed, You know how anxiously this soul searches for You, an effort no less than that which the bride of the book of Songs undertook. Just like that holy bride, this soul also roams madly about the public streets and plazas, praying and beseeching the daughters of Jerusalem to tell it where the Beloved is: "I adjure you, O daughters of Jerusalem, if you find my beloved, tell him this: I am faint with love" (Song 5:8).

In this state, how well my soul understands what is written in the Psalms: *"Deficit spiritus meus.... Deficit in salutare tuum anima mea."*[5]

You alone see the affliction of the soul that seeks You, and yet, O my Lord, the soul would peacefully bear this affliction for Your love if only it knew that it is not abandoned by You, O Font of eternal bliss!...

Ah! You understand how cruel a martyrdom it is for this soul to see the great offenses the children of man commit in these most miserable and saddest of times, the horrible ingratitude with which You are repaid for Your loving promises, and the little or no thought that these truly blind people give to having lost You.

---

5. Ps 84:2 "My soul longs, indeed it faints...."; Ps 118:81 "My soul languishes for your salvation."

My God, my God! It is fitting to say that these people no longer trust in You since they so rudely deny You the tribute of their love. Alas! My God, when will that moment come when this soul sees the restoration of Your reign of love?… When will You put an end to my torment?…

O holy souls, you who are free of all anguish and already delight in the flood of supreme sweetness in heaven, how I envy your happiness! Alas! For pity's sake, you who are so close to the Fountain of life, you who see that I am dying of thirst in this base world, quench my thirst with a sip of that cool water.

Ah! Too poorly, O fortunate souls, I confess that I have spent my portion much too poorly, that I have guarded a jewel of such great value much too poorly, but, long live God, I feel there is still a way to remedy this failure.

And so, O blessed souls, be so kind as to help me, since I have not been able to find Him whom my soul needs, neither at rest nor at night. I, too, will arise like the bride of the sacred songs and search for Him who loves my soul: *"Surgam et quaeram quem diligit anima mea."*[6] I will search for Him at all times, I will search for Him in all things, and I will not stop until I have found Him on the threshold of his Kingdom…

O God! O God! Where are my thoughts leading me? What will happen to Your unhappy children, still my brethren, who perhaps already deserve Your thunderbolts? Indeed, You know, O my sweet Redeemer, how many times the memory of Your sweet countenance, indignant toward my unfortunate brethren, turned my blood to ice out of fear greater than the thought of eternal torments and all the pains of hell.

---

6. Song 3:2: "I will seek him whom my soul loves."

I have always implored You, and tremble as I entreat You now, that through Your mercy You might withdraw Your disapproving glance from my unhappy…. You said yourself, O my sweet Lord, that "love is strong as death and as fierce as hell," (cf. Song 8:6). Therefore, look with an eye of ineffable sweetness on these my dead brethren[7]; bind them to Yourself with a powerful bond of love.

May all of these truly dead souls rise up again, O Lord! O Jesus, Lazarus made no request at all for You to raise him from the dead. What sufficed for him were the prayers of a sinful woman.[8] Ah, then, O my divine Lord, here is another soul, also sinful and guilty beyond comparison, that prays for so many dead brethren who do not bother in the least to pray to You to raise them again.

You know, O my God and King, the cruel martyrdom these Lazaruses cause me. Call out to them with so powerful a cry as to give them life, and may they, upon your command, come out of the tomb of their immoral pleasures.

Do this, O Lord, so that all will bless the richness of Your mercy…

Alas! My father, I just realized that I have not been speaking but writing. O please forgive and pity one who is sick with an illness of the heart, and all the more because the illness that affects me is incurable.

You yourself exhort me to offer myself as victim to the Lord for the sake of poor sinners. I made this [offering] once and continue to renew it many times a day. But how is it that the Lord does not hear me? For their well-being I

_____

7. Padre Pio speaks here of spiritual death as the result of sin.

8. Cf. Jn 11:22ff.

have even offered my own life, and yet the Lord allows me to continue living.

Therefore, was the holocaust I made and continue to make of myself not pleasing to the Lord?

I am most appreciative, O father, for your proposal; let us unite in purpose and help one another. During poor weather, I can be found before the Lord from 4:30 in the morning until 9:30 A.M., and during the day, no matter the weather, from 10:45 P.M. until the Hail Mary.

These are my normal hours; the rest depends on circumstances. I have understood this act of reciprocal charity in general, but not really well. Be so kind as to help me to better understand it.

And now I am ready to answer your questions.

You first ask if that soul[9] should have confided to its confessors from the very beginning the work Jesus was doing in and outside this soul.

Rest assured even on this account, O father, because the soul of which we speak never maliciously kept silent with its spiritual directors, but [perhaps] with its confessors, about what was happening. I say with its confessors rather than spiritual directors because, unfortunately, its life being of the itinerant type, it was never able to meet, in the world especially, confessors enlightened in the ways of the supernatural.

I will express more clearly my thought on this matter during the first meeting I have with you.

Your second question: When did the martyrdom of scruples begin in this soul, how long did it last, and where was it during that time?

---

9. Once again, Padre Pio speaks of himself (that soul) in the third person.

This was very a painful martyrdom for the poor thing because of its intensity and duration. If I remember correctly, it began when the soul was about 18 years old, and lasted until it was 21. However, during the first two years the martyrdom was almost unbearable.

The soul was at St. Elia's[10] and then St. Mark's,[11] among other places, when it was going through this ordeal.

The third question is whether this soul continues to receive communications from unidentified souls of whom it has no knowledge.

It has been some time since these communications reached this soul directly.

The fourth question is if Jesus showed signs of returning this soul to its resting place.

Jesus has not manifested anything in this regard, but the poor thing hopes so and has faith that this hope will not be disappointed.

Regarding that soul you asked about elsewhere, Jesus has not revealed anything further. May Jesus be ever blessed for all of eternity!

Do not worry about the state of your spirit. I beg you only to keep watch with more keen attention to the movements of your heart. Before all else, let us humble ourselves always in the presence of the majesty of the Lord, from whose presence we seek never to depart. And let us always remain vigilant so as not

---

10. After his novitiate, Padre Pio completed his studies in humanities at this monastery: January 1904–October 1905, and April 1906–October 1907.

11. Padre Pio completed a year of philosophy (October 1905–April 1906) in this monastery. He then took a course on theology at Serracapriola and Montefusco in October 1907.

to allow the demon to creep into us through the sin of vain-glory.

I do not know if I have satisfied your just demands, and, to the contrary, I dare to beg that so much care not be spent on my behalf.

I end here, O father, because I am tired due to a latent flu that has been troubling me for some days now. In the meantime, let it please Jesus to keep us united in spirit and always in his presence.

I recommend my poor soul to you and all those that are close to my heart, and pray more than ever for poor Raffaelina and her sister.

Greatly bless your poor, humble son at every moment.

FRA PIO, CAPUCHIN

Pardon me, father, if I ask a rather indiscrete question: Am I able to obtain the plenary indulgences as detailed on our calendar?

~ *3* ~

"I have never trusted in myself."

In this letter we find the recurrent theme of the soul's union with God through "pure faith," a fundamental idea for Padre Pio. The holy man seems most himself when speaking of his soul being united with his Creator [314].

[Pietrelcina, end of January 1916][12]

~

I.M.I.D.F.C.

My dearest father,

May Jesus always be with you and give you a clear understanding of my true interior state at present, which I am prepared to speak to you about. So be it.

I take advantage of the briefest instants, when I am allowed to re-enter myself, to find the reason for my desolation and to transcribe for you in this letter as much of it as is within my power.

---

12. With no place of origin and date included, this letter was found in the same envelope with a letter dated February 27. It is evidently Padre Pio's reply to Father Agostino's letter of January 20 to which Father Agostino refers in his letter on January 29.

For a long time my soul has found itself immersed day and night in the deep night of the spirit. My spiritual darkness lasts for long hours, for days on end, and often for entire weeks.

When I am in this night, I could not tell you if I am in hell or in purgatory. The intervals when a little light is shed upon my spirit are fleeting. Meanwhile, in this state I then wonder at the account to be made of my life, and in a flash I feel myself falling into this dark prison cell and I instantly lose the remembrance of all the Lord's generous favors to my soul.

Then it is farewell to the delights with which the Lord once inebriated the soul! Where is the enthusiasm with which it once relished that adorable divine Presence? Everything, everything has disappeared from the intelligence, from the soul. An endless desert of darkness, of despondency, of numbness is the birthplace of death, the night of abandonment, the cave of desolation. This is where my poor soul finds itself far from God and all alone.

Continuous is the sighing of the soul under the weight of this night, which surrounds it completely, that penetrates it completely. But it considers itself not only incapable of thinking of supernatural things, but of the most ordinary as well. And when the soul is just about to grasp a single ray of the Divine, all light suddenly vanishes from its sight.

It feels its will-power escaping; it strives to love, but in a flash, my father, it finds itself hardened and as firm as a rock. It searches its memory to try to attach itself to anything that could console it, but everything, everything is futile.

Is this not an appalling state?

But that's not all, my father. What increases my torment all the more is the vague memory of having at other times known and loved the Lord. I now feel that I no longer know Him or love Him; the Lord is just an unidentified, absent person, a complete stranger to me.

So I keep forcing myself to try to find a trace of the One my soul desires at least in His creatures. But who can say? I no longer recognize even there the usual image of the One who has forsaken me. It is at this very moment that the soul, defeated by fear and terror and no longer knowing how to find its God, goes about exclaiming and challenging its Lord, "God, my God, why have you forsaken me?"[13]

But what a horrible fright! There is no voice, not even an echo, to respond in this void the soul feels within itself. But not even this causes the soul to give up. It attempts to make new efforts, but always in vain. Then it feels drained of all warmth; it feels all its strength gone; it sees all feelings of pity completely abated.

Torn from its Bridegroom, cut to the depths of its most hidden being, this soul knows not what else to do in this deepest night. And my supplication grows all the more intense because it seems that these intolerable ills will endure forever. The poor soul sees no end whatsoever to this horrible misery. A wall of bronze seems to be enclosing me in this horrid prison forever.

So many and acute are the pains felt here that I am at a loss to say how I would suffer any differently if I were in hell. On the contrary—permit me to say this—here, in this state, one must suffer even more because of the love with which one loves the Creator. But let's move on.

It seems to me that when one is at the height of this martyrdom, the soul tries to console itself with the thought that in the end it must necessarily succumb to the weight of such

---

13. See Mt 27:46; Mk 15:34.

sorrows, because it is absolutely impossible to tolerate them longer.

But long live God! For the thought of the immortality that resists hell is suddenly presented to the soul about to be lost. Then the soul feels it still permeates a living body, and is about to invoke another's aid when it at once feels its cry being suffocated...and here I become mute and I cannot say what happens to me then.

These things are not at all new, and there is no language to describe them. All I will say is that this is precisely the height of my pains, and I do not know whether or not I please the Lord. As for me, I try to love Him, I desire Him, but in this night of darkest shadows my blind spirit wanders, my heart is dried up, my strength beaten down, my senses exhausted.

I go about struggling, I sigh, weep, moan, but all in vain. Prostrate with sorrow and devoid of strength, the poor soul submits to the Lord saying, *"Non mea, o dulcissime Iesu, sed tua voluntas fiat."*[14]

There you have it, O my dearest father, my interior laid bare. I would like to seek your assistance, but I am well aware that no one can relieve such profound anguish, which I cannot even express to myself and that no one is capable of understanding unless he has experienced it.

I received your letter and I do not know whether to hide from you the wonder, or better, my regret at certain questions you ask. And, to tell the truth, I wept a great deal over it. May the divine will be done, for thus He wills to try me. Even poor Job, as God permitted, received hostility not comfort from his friends.

---

14. "Not my will, O sweetest Jesus, but your will be done," cf. Lk 22:42.

I understand that the case is not going well for whatever reason, but God alone knows what is happening to me. What I wrote from Foggia to that soul is true, but I am not allowed to state names here in writing. If we are given the chance to see each other again, I will relate everything.

I have never trusted in myself; I can state before my conscience that I never took a step without the advice of another, and as for the steps already taken I always reconsidered, always asked for new insight from as many people as I happened upon.

I am sorry to have to return the charitable alms you sent me only because my present physical health will make it most difficult for me to celebrate [Mass] for an entire month without interruption.

May the good Jesus repay you and the principal giver, whoever that might be, for such extravagant charity.

Bless me heartily in every moment and may Jesus remain with us forever.

[FRA PIO]

"My father, how difficult it is to believe!"

Written from Foggia in 1916, this letter begins the second period that divides Padre Pio's Letters. Penetrated by a rich intuition of a theology of the act of faith, Padre Pio is aware that in believing there may be fears, shadows, some uncertainties regarding the revealed content, but there absolutely cannot be doubts. This helps us to understand his enigmatic allusion to the awakening of passions "with the exception of one," as meaning doubts of faith [326].

Foggia, March 8, 1916

·◇·

J.M.J.D.F.C.

My dearest father,

May Jesus be with you always and with all the souls that love Him with purity of heart. So be it.

I would like at least once, O father, for my letters to bring a smile and joy to you. But that is not within my power, even more so at the present time. Peace has been fully banished from my heart. I have become completely blind. I find myself enveloped in a profound darkness and I can never, no matter how I struggle, find the light.

How can I, therefore, walk well before the Lord? Ah! No, He can never be happy with me. Justly, He has thrust me among the eternal dead whom He has forgotten. It was my wickedness that heaped so much misfortune upon me. But tell me frankly, can I hope for a better day when the Lord, in His extreme goodness, will be indulgent toward me?

Amid the surrounding night I always fix my eyes on the east, so as to make out that miraculous star which once guided our fathers to the grotto of Bethlehem. But in vain do I turn my eyes to see the rising of that luminous astral body. The longer I look, the weaker my vision grows. The more I force myself, the more ardently I search, the more I see myself enveloped in greater gloom. I am alone by day, I am alone by night, and no ray of light enters to illuminate me. Never does a drop of relief come to quicken the flame, which continuously devours without consuming me.

I felt only once, in the most secret and intimate part of my spirit, something so delicate I do not know how to describe it. At first the soul felt His presence without seeing it, and then, I would say, He drew so near the soul that it felt His touch fully—just as when one body touches another, to give you a pale comparison. I do not know what else to say except to confess that I was overcome by the greatest fright at first, and shortly afterward this fright was changed to heavenly ecstasy. It seemed to me that I was no longer an exile and I cannot say whether I was aware of still being in my body when this happened. Only God knows, and I just do not know what to say to make you understand this event.

But, dear God, who could have imagined what was about to happen! All hell broke loose! This says it all. I was thrown into a prison darker than the previous one. This is where I find myself at present and nothing but perpetual horror reigns here.

Here all sins are laid bare and the soul sees nothing but its malice, in the highest degree of intensity, and, at the same time, it sees clearly how completely and absolutely far it is from that union with God to which it continually aspires.

The soul does not doubt the mercy of the Lord, who might one day unite it to Himself; rather, here where everything is completely subjective, the soul finds in itself the impossibility of such a union. It perceives in itself qualities that are in complete contradiction to that union.

Imagine then if there can be any consolation for this soul. It sees itself cast away from the face of the Lord and finds this entirely just. It sees clearly that its loss is irreparable. It does not know how to reconcile itself to so great a loss. It desires to love the God by whom it sees itself repelled. Indeed, it forces itself to love Him and its only thought, which torments it at every instant, is to love this God, whom it has so offended. It wants to love Him despite everything, and even though it sees its loss as irreparable.

To all this must be added the awakening of all the passions, with the exception of one. An infinite number of fears assail me at every instant. Temptations regarding faith want to drive me to deny everything. My father! How difficult it is to believe! May the Lord help me not to cast a shadow of doubt over what it has pleased God to reveal to us. I long for death to relieve me of my afflictions. May the Lord God grant me this soon, because I can endure no longer.

I would like, O father, to continue communicating and opening myself up to that person who, by now, knows how to bear with my sorrow, but I cannot go on. My hand is trembling and cannot keep a grip on my pen; I feel my throat contracting with sobs.

I await a long letter from you, in which I will hear myself inexorably condemned. The impact that will reverberate in me will certainly be horrible, but, if nothing else, I will have the satisfaction—if that is even possible—of for once being right in the end. I wager that you will be convinced this time of the reality of these things and will finally change your opinion.

Be so kind as to present my sincerest regards to the most dear father lector, and may you both give my case careful consideration, so that at least one of you might think me right for once.

I kiss your hand with the greatest respect, humbly praying that you will bless him who also offers himself,

your poor son,

FRA PIO

Do not become angry with your son for daring to reopen this letter. I give you free reign to speak with me a bit about the last confession I made to you. Therefore, between what I said then and what I have exposed in this current letter, combined with what I have said to you on innumerable occasions, you can render more precise judgment on my condition. In my last confession I told you that the darkness by which I am assailed is such that it causes me doubt, or better that I find it impossible to discern what is good from what is not.

How should I act so as not to offend the Lord? It is true that you gave me a directive on this point, but what can I say? I do not remember exactly what it was. Please be indulgent and show some charity by sending it to me in writing.

·∾· *5* ·∾·

"When will the sun rise within me?"

The immediate and principal reason for Padre Pio's return to the monastery, after a period of time with his family in Pietrelcina, was to give spiritual assistance to Raffaelina Cesare. She is the person Padre Pio refers to at the end of this letter, written a week before Raffaelina's death on March 25, 1916. [42].

Foggia, March 17, 1916

·∾·

I.M.I.D.F.C.

My dearest father,

May Jesus always be with you and with all the souls that love Him with heartfelt purity and sincerity. So be it.

I received your last letter at the same time that I received father provincial's, and I praise our God for everything, for your most delicate charity, and I offer most fervent thanks and eternal gratitude for you.

From the few things written to father provincial, you can gather the state of my soul—not to mention my present spiritual state—in the face of your affirmations and assurances. But long live Jesus, who in His pursuit of me does not allow the soul to be overcome by desperation, and this I believe only with the tip of my spirit without any comfort and without seeing, because of the assurances and affirmations both of you have given me.

In short, my belief is a total exercise of my poor will against all my human inclinations. Perhaps it is exactly for this reason that my faith never receives nourishment—neither in the senses nor the intellect. All in all, my belief is the result of the exertion of continual effort I impose on myself. And all of this, my father, is not a matter of only a few times a day, but it is continuous, or otherwise I could not help but become unfaithful to my God.

The night grows ever darker and I do not know what the Lord still has in store for me.

There are so many things I would like to say to you, O father, but I cannot. I recognize that I am a mystery even to myself.

When will the moment come when the mists of my soul fall away? When will the sun rise within me? Can I hope for it in this world? I believe it will never come to pass.

But enough of that; I realize what I am saying could make you incredulous, thus the fear of irritating you makes me prefer silence. In the meantime, commend me incessantly to the Lord and implore Him that belief in Him not be so difficult for me.

What can I possibly give to those souls that pray for me and offer themselves as victims of atonement? I pray continually for them, but what good is the prayer of someone who is always rejected by God? *Fiat voluntas Dei!* Let God's will be done! I trust and do not despair.

Assure that privileged soul of Jesus' delight in her. May she live in peace and be adorned for new battles, which the divine Father will clarify for her later, because of the pure delight he takes in her.

As for her sister, tell her that she finds herself in spiritual infancy, that Jesus has great plans for her, and that she should prepare herself to enter into another state of life.

And you then, force yourself to control the anxieties of your heart. Have confidence and calm in the great work of your own holiness and in the holiness of others. The rest is up to Jesus.

For quite awhile now Raffaelina has been on the cross of delight; she suffers with invincible resignation. For my part, it torments me to see her in such a state. Perhaps I will have to allow her to sing the *Nunc dimittis*[15]; I feel weak and it is probably better to yield.

Whenever God wills, we will come to better terms on this point, which must certainly ring badly to the ear of one who is foreign to the situation....

Bless me always, while I cordially embrace you,

FRA PIO

---

15. "Master, now you are dismissing your servant..." are words found in the Gospel of Luke (2:29–32). Uttered by Simeon at the presentation of Jesus in the Temple, it is a prayer of petition, thanksgiving, and prophecy.

◆ *6* ◆

"I will always seek the company of all those who are lovers of Jesus."

Padre Pio's success in his pastoral activity is immediately evident in this "summer" letter. The very day after his arrival at Foggia, he is at the center of an intense spiritual movement and sought after as its director. Perhaps not everyone was aware of the teacher's responsibility or the scale of that movement. His transfer to the new monastery of San Giovanni Rotondo now appears imminent [350].

Foggia, August 23, 1916

◆

I.M.I.D.F.C.

My dearest father,

May Jesus always assist you and give you abundant strength to allow you carry out your sacred ministry with exactitude.

This year I would have liked to let your name day pass unobserved, but I did not succeed. Besides, how could I give you my best wishes when you are in the land of terror? I give you my wishes in the only way I know how and am able and, good as you are, please deign to accept them knowing that they come from a heart that loves you ardently with a completely holy love before the divine Bridegroom.

The most sincere wish I extend to you, for such a strange day as this, is that the good God might grant you His most select graces, with a most perfect correspondence to His will on your part.

Accept, my dearest father, these most ardent promises on your behalf during this year of extreme discomfort and utmost desolation. You can already comprehend how I spend this day before Jesus, and be sure that as soon as I am alone, I will struggle sweetly before Him.

I will always seek the company of all those who are lovers of Jesus, particularly those who are united with us in one and the same spirit. Yes, father, all of us pray for you always! May it please the heavenly Father to render all of us worthy of eternal glory, and thus we will release hymns of praise and benediction for all eternity.

If I do not give you my news more often, alas, father, please do not blame me; know that it is not due to poor intentions. You know everything. You must also know that a free moment is never afforded me; a throng of souls who thirst for Jesus so besiege me as to make me want to pull my hair out.

On the one hand I rejoice in the Lord before such an abundant harvest, because I see the lines of chosen souls growing ever longer and Jesus more loved. On the other hand, I feel overcome by such a burden and almost disheartened for many reasons that are easy to understand.

With a bit of relief and relaxation in mind, I asked father provincial to send me again to San Giovanni for a while. I did not really express to him all the reasons that drove me to ask for his permission. I expressed only a few reasons and with great timidity. He answered right away, fully granting all I had asked of him. But he told me to wait a little longer until we know the fate that will befall father guardian,[16] who is presently undergoing experimental treatment at one of the military hospitals in Rome.

When he is released, father provincial said I can leave for San Giovanni as soon as he has returned. If he does not return, he added, I will have to wait until someone else comes along so that there will be two of us.

Tell me, father, was I perhaps wrong to seek this permission for the reasons only partly noted above? If this was wrong, I am willing to make whatever sacrifice in order not to fail the divine will.

I would like to tell you many things, but let that be done in better times. I no longer feel the strength to continue. May Jesus reward you for the good you have done for me, and, in the name of Jesus, I again embrace you filially and cordially.

FRA PIO, CAPUCHIN

Fra Paolo and Fra Camillo[17] are getting better and better. Please accept their most respectful regards.

---

16. Father Nazarene of Arpaise.

17. Brother Camillo of San Giovanni Rotondo, born on March 7, 1892, a soldier in World War I, was ordained a priest on September 8, 1922. He died on November 3, 1957.

"Obedience is everything for me."

With a Franciscan modesty bordering on the incredible, the young Pio expresses almost a fear of being "a cross" to his spiritual director. Pio is at odds with himself in his desire to obey Father Agostino because obedience gives him no comfort, and yet he knows that obedience is his only hope for salvation and to be able "to sing of victory" [351].

Foggia, August 26, 1916

·◌·

J.M.J.D.F.C.

My dearest father,

May the grace of Jesus always be in your heart and give you the strength to withstand the trials to which He subjects you!

Only a few words this time not because I do not feel the need, but, in fact, because I cannot coordinate my thoughts at all. I feel poorly, physically and morally. Comfort no longer descends into my heart and the storm grows in intensity.

I live only to obey you, the good God having made me understand this to be the one thing He welcomes most, and the only way for me to hope for health and to sing of victory. But, my father, what objections I feel! It is true I do not feel within me a rebellion against the one who governs me, but I experience a certain anxiety that makes me feel badly.

In short: obedience is everything for me, and I do not find any comfort in subjecting myself to obedience. May God protect me if, with eyes wide open, I should in the least way go against he who was assigned to judge me internally and externally. Yet, how is it that I am full of fears regarding this point? Tell me, for heaven's sake, what am I supposed to do?

When, then, will the Lord completely remove from you the cross to which He has subjected you? I pray for this always. I continually renew my offering to Jesus on your behalf. What else should I do? Offer me to Jesus so that He might make you happy.

In the meantime, you need not impose on yourself concern about my weakness. Jesus will help me! Besides the sacrifices I have already made and always renew, I am ready, most ready to make hundreds more even more painful sacrifices.

Father Isaiah[18] is already here. I await your renewal of the obedience so that I can go to San Giovanni.

That soul from Morra Irpino[19] has already written to me seeking direction. She even tells me that before leaving San Marco she asked your permission to write to me. Meanwhile, what do you say regarding this?

---

18. Father Isaiah of Sarno, born in 1889, served as a medic during the war from 1915 to 1918. He stopped at the monastery at Foggia during a temporary leave, making it possible for Padre Pio to go to San Giovanni Rotondo.

19. The village of Morra Irpino, now Morra De Satinis (Avellino), is located 64 kilometers from the county seat and has a population of 2,739. The "soul" that has corresponded with Padre Pio and asked for spiritual direction is a young woman, Maria Gargani, then a teacher at the school of San Marco la Catola. She had entered the third order Franciscans, but desired to consecrate herself to God through religious vows. Padre Pio did not believe this God's will for her. Later, in February 1936, Maria Gargani founded a congregation of women religious: the Apostle Sisters of the Sacred Heart.

As for Father Agostino, he has already given me permission. I await an answer for everything.

I kiss your hand. Pray for me and bless me always.

Your most obedient son,

FRA PIO, CAPUCHIN

·❧· *8* ·❧·

"Will you show yourself one day on Tabor at the hour of the holy sunset?"

The first part of this letter is a heartfelt prayer addressed to the Trinity. Padre Pio, certainly having in mind the meeting of God and Moses on Mount Sinai, turns to the omnipotent Father amidst his fire among thorns and offers himself as a son in the Only-begotten Son of God. The holy man fervently wishes to move beyond a mystical vision, albeit one of "thick gloom," to a physical vision. The allusion to a sunset without first mentioning a dawn is unusual [368].

San Giovanni Rotondo, November 8, 1916

·❧·

J.M.J.D.F.C.

My dearest Father,

May Jesus always help you and give you light to understand my present state.

May Jesus always test me with the fire of suffering: *Fiat!* Now we are in the midst of the trial heralded to me in Foggia.[20] For some time now, my good father, I have felt within me the

---

20. On August 13, Padre Pio wrote from Foggia to Father Benedetto: "He (Jesus) tells me that it is necessary to comfort the body a little in order to ready myself for other trials, to which He wishes to subject me."

strong need to turn to you for some words of comfort in the midst of storms where my poor soul found itself as soon as you departed. But it was not possible until this present moment, so turbulent is the storm within and without me.

My God, what my life has been in these days! The thickest darkness has clothed everything! And what is my future to be? I know nothing, absolutely nothing. Meanwhile, I will not cease raising my hands toward the sacred place through the darkness, and I will always praise You as long as I have a breath of life.

I implore you, O my good God, to be my life, my ship, and my port. You have made me ascend the cross of Your Son and I try to adapt to the best of my ability. I am convinced that I will never descend from that cross and that I will never again see the air calm around me.

I am persuaded of the necessity of speaking to You amid the thunder and turbulence; I must see You in the briers, amid the fiery thorns. But to do this, I see that it is necessary for me to remove my shoes and to renounce my own will and affections entirely.

I am disposed for everything, but will You show Yourself one day on Tabor at the hour of the holy sunset? Will I have the strength, without ever tiring, to ascend toward the celestial vision of my Savior?

I feel that the ground on which I walk is giving way under my feet. Who will strengthen my steps? Who if not You, who are the staff in my weakness? *Miserere,* O God, have mercy on me! No, do not make me experience my weakness any longer!

May the light of faith illuminate my intellect once again, Your charity warm my heart shattered by the pain of offending You in the hour of trial! My [God], how horrible is this thought that never leaves me! My God, my God, do not make me suffer this agony for You any longer! I can bear it no longer!

My father, forgive me! I no longer know how to order my thoughts. If I had not been interrupted, who knows where I would have gone. Without my realizing it, I would have put your patience to a severe test.

Be so kind as to listen to my present state, which I promise to reveal briefly. The battle has been renewed with more fury. For many days my spirit has been immersed in the thickest darkness. I acknowledge that I find myself in a state of the greatest inability to do good. I find myself in extreme abandonment: greatly distressed in my spiritual appetite, I experience bitterness in my inner mouth that renders this world's sweetest wine most bitter.

Blasphemous thoughts continuously run through my mind; and still more promptings, infidelity, and irreligiousness. I feel my soul pierced through; I die every moment that I live. My soul no longer rests peacefully in God's, for surely He would not allow what is happening within me unless He was greatly displeased with me. He cannot find Himself in this soul again. He is too pure and would be very uncomfortable remaining in a soul where such things take place.

The demon creates a din and roars incessantly around my poor will. I do nothing in this state except say with steady resolve, but without feeling: *Long live Jesus!* I believe... But who can tell you how I utter these holy expressions? I utter them with timidity, without strength and courage, and I must do great violence to myself.

Tell me, father, is it possible that this condition is compatible with God's presence in the soul? Is this not perhaps the result of God's withdrawal? My father, I pray you, speak to me again with complete candor and sincerity. Advise me on the way I must act so as not to offend the Lord and, if there is hope, so that God will return to this soul.

The thickest darkness still reigns over everything I do. With all of my actions a perpetual doubt crosses my soul. A feeling always tells me that I do everything with a doubtful conscience. I try to remember what obedience has directed on this matter, but what do you want! The Lord confuses me; I remember nothing definite! What a torment even this constitutes for me! Not knowing if one works for God's glory or offense is more painful than death.

For heaven's sake, my father, do not become angry with me! I am ready for everything, to sacrifice everything, as long as I do not offend God. Be so kind, therefore, as to make some suggestion on this subject. Tell me how I must respond to these most painful thoughts prompted by I know not whom.

I would like to tell you so many things, but I cannot control myself. Immersed in this most painful state, I cannot put my thoughts in order. My heart wants to love; it strives to succeed at this, but does not find the way. The poor thing finds itself outside its center, and for this reason it does not know where it can rest.

My father, how much time remains before I am freed from this state? O! At least if I could know God is not offended by all of this. If I could know this, I feel disposed to bear the utmost suffering for my entire life, however long that might be.

Bless me always and pray that if my present state does not glorify Jesus, He may liberate me as soon as possible.

Despite all the torments I feel in the most intimate reaches of my spirit, I always feel the strength to pray for you and to continuously renew the offering I once made to God on your behalf.

With the greatest esteem and deep respect and veneration, I kiss your hand, calling myself always,

Your poor son,

FRA PIO, CAPUCHIN

When replying to this letter, I ask you to send one of your certificates, to be presented when I go in Naples, so that I might celebrate Mass.

"It is true that everything I am is consecrated to Jesus."

Padre Pio's physical pains increase as the stigmata draws near. Poor Padre Pio weeps "without wanting to, like a baby." He is alone. Apparently he speaks to no one of what is happening to him, not even the brothers with whom he lives under the same roof at San Giovanni Rotondo. His only communications are the letters to his spiritual director, written in the silence of his "cell" [388].

San Giovanni Rotondo, March 6, 1917

∞

J.M.J.D.F.C

My dearest Father,

May Jesus continue to own your heart entirely until you are transformed in the glory of the heavenly regions!

Your last letter[21]—brief but full of assurances and holy, loving advice—deeply touched my heart. It inspired me to promise once again that I will begin to truly love Jesus without anxiety, and that I will consecrate my entire life to His holy service again.

---

21. This letter is missing.

I feel very keenly the desire to spend every instant of my life in loving the Lord, though more often than not without ever thinking I can achieve this. I desire to remain ever so close to Him, to take hold of one of His hands and travel joyfully along that sorrowful path, the via dolorosa, upon which He has placed me. But—I say this with death in my heart, confusion in my soul, and my face blushing—my desires do not exactly correspond to reality.

A trifle is enough to agitate me; forgetting your assurances is enough to throw me into the arms of the darkest night of the spirit, which causes me to suffer agonies both night and day. My God! My father! What great punishment my past infidelities have brought upon me!

I would like to think of nothing other than Jesus, my heart to beat only and always for Jesus alone, and I continuously promise all of this to Jesus. But, alas! I am well aware that my mind goes astray or, more precisely, settles into the hardest trial to which the spirit is subjected, and the heart cannot help but decay in this pain.

It is true that everything I am is consecrated to Jesus and I intend to suffer everything for Him. But I cannot reconcile myself to this. I am entirely devoid of light and this is enough to fill me with terror and dread, to make me believe I am enduring the rigors of divine justice. In large measure what continually confirms me in this truth, in my opinion, is seeing God, who becomes larger and larger in the eyes of the spirit, growing further and further away, and that this God is more and more encircled by dense clouds.

My spirit is always firm in its purpose to the extent that this purpose is always in mind. The more I fix my gaze on Him, the more aware I become that He is hiding in that cloud that is like a mist rising from the ground at sunrise.

The heavenly Father still does not fail to allow me to partake, even physically, in the sufferings of his only-begotten Son. These pains are so intense that one can neither describe nor imagine them at all. I do not know if it is due to a lack of strength or sin that, when in this state, I weep without wanting to, like a baby.

A truly difficult trial is my not knowing whether God is pleased or offended by what I do. I have received many assurances in this matter, but what do you want! One does not have eyes to see. And then the enemy always wants to put his tail in the way to ruin everything. He keeps insinuating that such assurances do not embrace all my actions, much less at all times.

Alas, father! Speak again in this regard. Calm my poor spirit, beaten on every side. Think of me as a poor blind man in absolute need of your guidance. Do not abandon me, father. If you see me on the wrong path, do not spare me your condemnation, since I still hope at that point that the Lord would use His mercy toward me by placing me once again on the straight path leading to Him.

I excuse myself from telling you of the reasons for my last sustained crisis, knowing that Father Paolino has informed you of everything.

Now, then, I come to ask you a permission, certain that you will not deny me. I have a profound desire to offer myself as victim to the Lord for the perfection of this institution that I love tenderly and for which I spare no personal discomfort.

It is true that I have many reasons to thank the heavenly Father in the change for the better that has occurred in the majority of them [the boarders], but I am not yet fully satisfied.

Therefore, I beseech you not to deny me what I have asked. Jesus will give me the strength to bear another sacrifice.

Father, I beg you with tears in my eyes never to abandon me and to bless me always.

In expectation of one of your letters to soothe the storms that rage in my spirit, I kiss your hand, being always,

Your poor son,

FRA PIO, CAPUCHIN

Dearest father,

I am reopening this to notify you of the following: Father Paolino's mother, for reasons easy to understand, does not want Annita to stay in her home any longer. With the help of a priest from Casacalenda we have tried to have her received in the convent of the sisters of Larino,[22] but that was not possible.

The only door that remains open to her at the present is to have her accepted as a patient with the sisters here. The Mother Superior took upon herself the task of applying to the president of the charitable organization to set aside a place for her. The application was granted. Now what do we do? The decision is up to you.

I do not see clearly how she came here, but at present there is no other way out for that poor dear woman.

Once again, I kiss your hand.

---

22. The Apostle Sisters of the Sacred Heart of Jesus served at the seminary and hospital at Larino (Campobasso) in 1917.

∽ *10* ∽

"I feel my soul crushed by sorrow."

The progressive journey toward mystical union is always, and in general, accompanied by great physical and moral ordeals. Among these trials are often found prolonged and incurable illnesses and a tension between the hatred for and simultaneous delight in sin, accurately described by Padre Pio in this letter [408].

San Giovanni Rotondo, July 16, 1917

∽

J.M.J.D.F.C.

My dearest father,

May Jesus ever be the life of your heart, supporting it through every trial, transforming it into Himself!

You wish[23] to know clearly how my spirit is doing. But how do I describe what I am feeling? Please believe that it is in just this that the height of my internal torment consists. I live in continual night; the darkness is so very thick.

I aspire to the light and this light never comes. If at times a dim ray is glimpsed, which happens all too rarely, it is precisely this that reignites my soul's most desperate longing to see the sun shine again. And these longings are so great and so violent that

---

23. A reference to a missing letter.

they very often cause me to languish, to suffer an agony of love for God, and bring me to the verge of fainting.

I feel all of this without wanting to and without making any effort. Most of the time, all of this happens outside of prayer and even when I am busy with commonplace tasks.

I would like not to feel these things, because when they are quite violent I feel them even physically. I have a great fear that I am not meant for this sort of thing. It seems that I die at every instant, and I would like to die so as not to feel the heaviness of God's hand that weighs upon my spirit.

What could this be? How should I conduct myself to escape such a deplorable state? Is God at work in me or is there another who is acting? Speak to me clearly, as always, and let me know how all of this comes about.

What is more, at certain moments I am assaulted by violent temptations against faith. I am sure that my will does not rest in them, but my imagination is so ignited and presents these temptations in such bright colors that, wandering about my mind, the sin appears not only an indifferent matter but delightful.

From this are born all those thoughts of discomfort, diffidence, desperation, and even—for heaven's sake, father, do not be horrified—blasphemies. I am frightened in the face of so much strife. I tremble and do violence to myself, and I am certain that, by the grace of God, I do not give in.

Added to all of this is the dismal image of my past life, where I see nothing but my miseries and ingratitude to God. I feel my soul crushed by sorrow and an extreme confusion pervades me. Because of this, I feel as though I were under a heavy press in which all my bones are dislocated and ground up.

I feel this brutal process not only in the innermost part of my spirit, but also in my body. And here, too, I am assailed by the strong fear that perhaps God is not the author of this strange phenomenon, for if He were, how can one explain the disturbance in my physical being? I do not know if this is possible.

What is more, I am always assailed by doubt—which hounds me in everything—that what I am doing may not be to God's liking. It is true that you have spoken to me several times about this, but what can I do if, put to the bitter test, I forget everything? Or if I do remember, I do not remember anything precise and everything is a blur. Alas! For heaven's sake, be so kind as to put it all in writing for me once again.

God, then, grows greater in my mind's eye, and I always see Him, encircled by dense clouds on the horizon of my soul's sky. I feel Him close, but my longing for God makes me see Him ever farther away. And with the growth of these longings, God becomes more intimate with me. My God! What a strange thing!

Father, do not forget that you have a debt to pay to this religious family: to come and spend about ten days with us. I am offering promises so that this comes to pass as soon as possible.

The Recchia boy[24] has only one pair of shoes in good condition—the only daughters of a widowed mother! May he do, therefore, with this family as he sees fit so as to provide for patched shoes.

The boys cannot wait to leave for their novitiate.

I kiss your hand and call myself,

FRA PIO, CAPUCHIN

---

24. A pupil of the seminary. His grandfather was Pasquale Recchia (1859–1944), from San Marco la Catola, and his grandmother a Franciscan tertiary, Teresa Pantano.

·❧· *11* ·❧·

"We must always cling to God with perseverance."

It is impossible to understand the human person as "spirit" if not in communion with God. If the person lives, loves, and works with the fullness of his or her powers, all of this is from God. Thus Padre Pio views his own life. In the midst of "pitch-black darkness," he does not lose his hope that God will never betray the spirit of His beloved creature [411].

San Giovanni Rotondo, July 24, 1917

·❧·

I.M.I.D.F.C.

My dearest father,

May the grace of Jesus be with you always!

All right, my dearest father, it is high time that I wrote to you, even if, dear me, it will again be in a rush, since I can never find a convenient time. I do this only to thank you heartily for the beautiful, comforting, tireless news you have given me.

I am writing you again to tell you that in my prayers and in the holy Mass I continually ask many graces for your soul, but, in particular, for the holy and divine Love, who is everything for us. This is the honey, my dear father, in and with which all our affections and actions and sufferings must be sweetened.

My God! My good father! How happy the inner realm where this holy Love reigns! How blessed are the powers of our soul when they obey such a wise King! He does not permit serious sins or even a fondness for the slightest of these to live under His obedience and in His kingdom.

It is true that He often allows them to dock at the edge so as to train the internal virtues for battle and make them valiant. He even permits spies—venial sins and imperfections—to run here and there within His realm, but only to make known that without Him we would fall prey to our enemies.

Let us humble ourselves a little, my good father, and confess that if God were not our armor and shield we would be thoroughly riddled with every type of sin. And it is for this reason that we must always cling to God with perseverance in our practices. May this be our persistent concern.

We always have the flame of charity afire in our hearts and we never lose courage. If some languor or weakness of spirit overtakes us, let us run to the foot of the cross, let us be seized by heavenly perfumes, and undoubtedly we will be reinvigorated.

During the holy Mass, I always present your heart to the divine Father and to His heavenly Son—He cannot refuse because of their union; that is exactly why I present my offering to God in this manner. I do not doubt, my dear father, that you do the same.

I was very happy to see you again with Father Pietro,[25] and I send infinite praises to the heavens for the grace Jesus gave you. Have you noticed, father, how poor his health is? May it please

---

25. Father Pietro of Ischitella.

Jesus to keep him with us. I always say this to Jesus, since I love Father Pietro a lot.

The trials of my spirit continue to intensify. But, I praise God who, even in the midst of my trials, does not permit my soul to become lost. There is suffering, but I have the certainty that in the pitch-black darkness in which my spirit is continually immersed, my hope does not fade.

I end here, father, by reassuring you that all the souls belonging to Jesus are holding up well and fighting valiantly. For you I wish the height of Christian perfection within the very womb of Jesus, and in Him, I, together with our boys, kiss your hand, and I ask, for myself and for them, your blessing.

Most affectionately, your son,

FRA PIO, CAPUCHIN

Father Paolino[26] sends his cordial regards. The most reverend father[27] has been in Foggia for many, many days, and he will probably return after St. Anne's. Vico's boys have been here for about a month, and those among ours who will go to the novitiate are still here. They are so very good. The imminent separation saddens me.

---

26. Father Paolino of Casacalenda.

27. Father Luigi of Serracapriola.

∾ *12* ∾

"To love my God is the effect of full knowledge."

In this letter, the intimacy between Padre Pio and his spiritual director is clear, but so, too, is the state of spiritual suffering that is taking over Padre Pio's soul. This suffering is associated with the fear of not fulfilling the will of God entirely. Note that Pio speaks to Father Benedetto as to a close friend who knows him in the smallest details of his deepest inner life [490].

San Giovanni Rotondo, June 19, 1918[28]

∾

I.M.I.F.

My dearest father,

May Jesus continue His holy love in you, may He make it grow in your heart, transforming it into Himself!

---

28. This letter has no place of origin or date. Father Benedetto wrote on the envelope: "1917?" Without doubt the letter was written from San Giovanni Rotondo on June 19, 1918. In fact, Padre Pio refers to it in another letter of the same date, which also appears on the signed copy sent to Father Agostino that same day. The text addressed to Father Agostino contains a few slight variations—indicated by *A.* in footnotes—and omits the last part of what Pio wrote to Father Benedetto.

I always offer this prayer before Jesus on your behalf. Now, more than ever, I repeat it with all the outpouring of my soul for your sake.

May it please God to grant this along with the other prayers I offer for you. But alas! How can he, who has become the object of the Most High's just vengeance, hope for graces?

I now gather up my soul's scattered powers to put down on paper, if possible, all the inner martyrdom[29] my soul, deprived of Goodness, now feels. But, O God! None of these powers answer. O God, how unfortunately true is what You say through the mouth of your psalmist: *"Nisi Dominus aedificaverti domum, in vanum laboraverunt qui aedificant eam."*[30] O my father, my father, the wandering spirit escapes my search and disappears in desolate wastes, as does that search it undertakes and feels in attempting to again draw near to at least the idea of my God.

Alas![31]... O heavens!... Where is my life? The sun that once looked indifferently on me suddenly knocks me down and frightens me, and I instinctively ask for a refuge to hide myself from my very self, were it possible, and from the just Lord who is angry with me. I would like to hide myself from everything, because it seems to me that even inanimate creatures[32] can read the condemnation and reproof written on my forehead, on my disgraceful face.[33]

---

29. In Father Agostino's letter, he omits: *inner martyrdom.*

30. Ps 127:1: "Unless the LORD builds the house, those who build it labor in vain."

31. A., omited.

32. A., he omits: *the inanimate creatures.*

33. A., he omits: *on my forehead.*

O heavens!… O life… What view[34] you take from me! Do you not know that without you, I am deprived of my very existence, that I cannot live any longer? O my father, only in keeping my soul restrained and closed off from everyone in silence; only in hiding myself from all creatures do I in some way manage not to rack my brains over my interior martyrdom.

But this loathsome book is ever open, and creatures, like the Creator, are always present. Therefore, the very sight of them brings forth from him sharp cries of the overwhelming necessity of this[35] as well as the clamor of persistent insomnia and abstinence from Him.[36]

I suffer in this drifting which I do not will; I tremble and I fear[37] that my cries and folly are harmful to the conformity demanded by the divine will and obedience. And because of this, failing to halt the dizzying course down that slope I do not wish to descend, exposing myself results in a double martyrdom: from my sufferings and from my very needs.

I abhor such work and I am tempted to destroy this letter[38] so that none of my news will reach you. The shamefulness of this creature, his hardheadedness, the outcast God has made him, all render him undeserving of any aid or direction.

Everything is devoured by a hidden force that consumes after a momentary relief or, rather, a simple and short-lived wakefulness. And so the value of counsel and direction are

---

34. A.: *vision*.

35. That is, *vision*.

36. In Father Agostino's letter we read: *In opening the loathsome book, in appearing before creatures, and the sharp cries of the overwhelming need for God come without any other reaction.*

37. A.: *fearing*.

38. A., he adds: *of mine*.

destroyed by the increased damage, of which the Lord will ask an account.

O my father, do not abandon this ungrateful soul to God. Do not reject this blind man, who has tread holy joys underfoot in order to cherish and feed upon what is foul! O God, I look upon this and tremble at such a dreadful sight! I seek [the Lord], my father, from the gloomy precipice from which I see myself tumbling. And if I sometimes seem to recover Him, He escapes me. Then I find nothing, I recover nothing, and I hang my tired arms in dejection; in vain the soul's excitement in seeking his Goodness. What torment, what martyrdom, what hell for the poor, dear soul!

Where will I find my God? Where can I place this poor heart that I feel bursting inside my chest? I am looking for Him with perseverance, but I do not find Him. I knock at the heart of the divine Prisoner and He does not answer me. What can this possibly mean? Has my unfaithfulness made Him so inflexible?[39] Can I possibly hope for mercy and that He at last will listen to my cries? Or must I renounce this hope? O God, may my horrid obstinacy be finally smashed. My only Good! May I finally love You with that love You require; may I finally come back to You from this breathless and heartrending search.[40]

My father, naked and squalid is my spirit; arid and dry is this heart for its God.[41] My spirit and heart show almost no more movement toward Him, who, in His goodness, created them. I almost[42] no longer have faith. When the tempest rages at its

---

39. A.: *severe*.

40. A., he omits: *May I come back…search.*

41. A.: *for God*.

42. A., he omits: *almost*.

height and the overflowing measure of my misery crushes me, I am powerless to raise myself on the wings of hope, so necessary for abandonment in God. I do not have charity. Ah! That to[43] love my God is the effect of full knowledge in an operative faith, and in whose promises the soul plunges, finds restoration, abandons itself, and rests in sweet hope. I do not have charity[44] toward my neighbor, because this is a consequence of the former, and lacking the first, from which every vital sap flows, every branch perishes.

Yes, I am devoid of everything, O my father, even of the larva of virtue, such that this condition seems to me one of mortal tepidness and, as such, God justly casts me out of His heart all the more.[45] I see that my ruin is irreparable and I see no way out.[46] Alas! I have lost every way, every means, every support, and every norm; and if I try to wake my dormant memory, a inexplicable dispersion takes place and I find myself more bewildered than before,[47] more powerless to raise myself up again, and the mysterious darkness grows thicker.[48]

My God, why is it that you shake and wound, shake still again and distress, with such violence,[49] this miserable soul, this soul already destroyed and whose destruction, they say, was stirred, caused, and willed by your command and permission?

---

43. A., he omits: *Ah! That.*

44. A., he adds: *charity.*

45. A.: cf. Rev 3:16.

46. A., he omits: *And I see…no way out.*

47. A.: *more bewildered, more powerless, and more in the dark than before.*

48. A., he omits: *to raise myself up again…thicker.*

49. A., he omits: *with such violence.*

Ah! My father, you who know Him, tell me, I beg you, and do not throw back in my face my dispersion,[50] my anxiety, and my wandering search for Him. Do not throw back in my face[51] the abandonment of this spirit that nevertheless longs for the most blind and humble rest by divine consent. Tell me, where is my God? Where might I find Him? What must I do to seek Him out? Tell me, will I ever find Him again? Tell me, where must I rest my heart that is extremely and mortally ill and which[52] I instinctively feel is[53] in a continuous, breathless, and painful search?

O God, O God, I cannot say more: Why have you abandoned me?[54] This spirit, justly stricken by your divine justice, remains amid such intense contradictions without any resource or sign but which[55] the short-lived glimmer of light that sharpens the pain and the martyrdom. I feel I am dying. I am burning with thirst. I languish with hunger, O father,[56] but it seems to me that my hunger is now being reduced to one sole longing for conformity to the divine will exactly as He wishes.

Yet, how is it that I always feel so agitated, so restless,[57] that it makes my insomnia and abandonment and the torture of the shock of my inability to understand the divine will so tormenting? No assurance succeeds in breaching the closed spirit except

---

50. A., he omits: *my dispersion.*

51. A., he omits: *do not throw back in my face.*

52. A., he omits: *extremely...which.*

53. *I feel is,* in A.: *is.*

54. A., he omits: *O God...abandoned me?*

55. A., he omits: *which.*

56. A., he omits: *O father.*

57. A., he omits: *so restless.*

for fleeting instants when the very novelty passes and flies away and just incites more hunger and thirst and the need for God.

But I always repeat *fiat,* and I long for nothing but the precise completion of this *fiat* in just the way God requires: generously and strongly. Ah, father, I ask you also[58] for the constant help of your prayer, because I find myself on the verge of being crushed, suffocated, and drowned[59] under such a difficult ordeal. I see hell opening beneath my feet[60] or, better yet, I have already descended there[61]: I am on the verge of failing.

Only the fear of offending my God again makes me shudder, and makes me suffer agonies to the point of death. I fear for my heart, unfortunately unaware as it is[62] of true evil. My iron intentions stand ready to obey blindly, but I fear some surprise to my heart[63]; may it not allow itself to be dragged along unbeknownst to my depressed will; and I suffer the pains of death in the doubt of transgressing the command of obedience, and displeasing my God even in the least.[64]

My father, there are so many things I still have to tell you. There are so many needs I have yet to expose to you, but I cannot. The sorrow that oppresses my spirit overcomes me and takes from me the ability to express myself.

---

58. A., he omits: *also.*

59. A., he omits: *suffocated, and drowned.*

60. A.: *under my feet.*

61. A., he omits: *or, better yet, I have already descended there.*

62. A., he omits: *as it is.*

63. A., he omits: *some surprise.*

64. A.: *in the least.*

I await your usual charity,[65] and send to the whole church my prayers and sacrifices on the feast of the Holy Apostles.

So here you have it, revealed as best as possible for me, the origin of my recent condition. O God! I cannot tell you, father, of the resistance and violence I had to undergo to reveal these things to you. I have revealed them to you by dint of will, in virtue of my obedience to you which demands that nothing must pass in silence. I have had to labor very hard to tear myself from Satan's clutches, and now I suffer his vengeance. He injects me continually with his poison and, at the mercy of his powers, it is impossible to find a way out when every path is closed and there is no glimmer of light to point to an escape.

My God! How long must I remain in this bloody state? My condition is simply desperate. Baser man manifests itself in all its abominable reality. I feel pity for my excessive misery.

My father, when will this slaughter-house end? It seems that every beauty of grace has been stripped from my soul. Deprived of this most essential adornment, and left to its own ability, it borders on being at the level of a beast.

Such knowledge presents itself to me vigorously in the entire scene of tendencies and attempts.

My God, pass the sentence and give me the strength to know how to suffer, and to suffer with love, the penalty for my guilt. And here, father, it seems I lack contrition. The "old man" reigns arrogantly and neither yields nor wishes to fall, and it

---

65. The letter addressed to Father Agostino ends in this way: *"I await your usual charity, and be assured that I never cease to present you to the Lord, even from this hell into which I have descended. I kiss your hand and ask for the comfort of your continual blessing. Your poor, humble son, fra Pio, Capuchin."*

seems to me that no effort is sufficient to bend this proud brow, which resists to the point of victory.

I perceive myself in such a state of ruin and I weep without finding strength enough to humble such haughtiness. The will is completely disgusted and neither knows how nor wishes to strengthen the spirit to pronounce, as it must, its *fiat* to this rejection.

How could all of this be? My day began May 29, and it continues declining. I feel crushed morally and physically, and it seems to me that I have not yet perceived the situation in all its terrorizing vision regarding my ministry.

So, battered, besieged, tedious…I throw myself on the altar with disgust and revulsion for the violence that accompanies me—monstrous and ugly. What happens in that awful mean-time, when I am at the altar, I cannot tell you because my soul feels without perceiving.

How can this be? Could it be a sacrilegious kiss when one truly feels life is dying and bleeding, and one's vital essence points to true condemnation? More often than not I do not know how to tell you whether or not I am outside the nobility of this act—lethargy seems to first accompany me and then to swallow me afterward.

O God! If I thought it were so, in that instant I would bow. Before a single sign was enough to make me fold at the altar. This lethargic sleep becomes complete in powerlessness and, always more tormenting and almost always followed by impetu-ousness in my efforts, by a complete captivity of the internal and external bodily senses.

Judge for yourself from what I was able to tell you if my state is not truly pitiable. I hope I was able to explain a subject so difficult, delicate, and very dangerous for me. I fear I deceive myself, revealing as truth what might not be true. My father, I put my trust in you that my soul may not be nourished on what is actually an illusion.

I draw this letter to a close, but with such pain and remorse! … It is well for the lowliest, most destitute, and contemptible to remain silent, and so I should be silent. If God's justice, which is right and holy and fitting, has struck me, what complaints should I voice?

My father, forgive me my stubbornness which compels me and which I cannot conceal. Bless me always, and do not neglect to continue helping me. Be assured that I pray for you regularly and I offer myself to God always. With profound respect, I kiss your hand.

Your poor, humble son,

FRA PIO, CAPUCHIN

This morning your postcard addressed to Father Paolino arrived. I think it is useless to mail it to him at Montefusco, because I do not know how long he will be there. I will deliver it to him upon his return and he will learn your wishes from it. In any case, you may send Bozzuto[66] and Grilli to Foggia on the third of the month, and they will find Father Paolino there.

Brother Carmine's[67] nephew, who is here, has to go to Vico.

---

66. Instead, only Luigi Bozzuto (Father Emmanuele of San Marco la Catola) went to Foggia from San Marco la Catola because Grilli had not yet reached the canonical age.

67. Brother Carmine of San Bartolomeo in Galdo, August 22, 1905—May 17, 1933.

I was told that the boy from San Giovanni failed his entrance exams for the academy. *Quid faciendum?*[68] Two more boys from here would also like to enter the academy and have reported passing their exams. But so far no one from the family has shown up.

---

68. What shall we do?

❧ *13* ❧

"Tell Jesus not to be tyrannical still."

Here is a remarkable sketch of the intimate confidence Padre Pio has in his spiritual director. In an openly mystical manner, this letter exposes the phenomena that preceded Padre Pio's stigmatization. He is very sincere when, overcome by the sorrow in his spirit and acting as one who is truly in love with Jesus, Pio asks his spiritual director to "tell Jesus not to be tyrannical again to the point that I come to tyrannize him myself" [496].

San Giovanni Rotondo, July 27, 1918

❧

J.M.J.D.F.C.

My dearest father,

May Jesus always continue His assistance and may He make you holy!

The tempestuous fury that shakes and howls around and within my spirit compels me to turn to you again ahead of time.... More unaware of my future than ever, surprised and frightened, full of worries, I run to you for some news, some sign of Him, and to learn what I must do to find Him again and to be admitted to His intimate embrace. What I am presently subjected to is horrible, and I feel crushed beneath a heavy millstone of such pain and torment.

In fact, these days my position is completely new—I should say the newest—such that I can in no way manage to express it, nor can my expression penetrate the depth of the intensity of deviations of the spirit, further astray than ever, scattered and abandoned.

Father! My God!!!... It is not for me to say more than this! This most acute martyrdom is the most my frailty can withstand. My spirit seems to ebb further away at each moment and is crushed by the repeated blows of divine justice, rightly angered by this wicked creature. My heart seems broken; it no longer even bleeds from the always increasing cruelty of this constant and merciless death.

My father! My God! I have lost every trace, every vestige of the highest Good in the strictest sense. All my frantic efforts in search of this Good have proven useless. I am alone in my search, alone in my emptiness and misery, alone in the vivid image of what could be, and alone even in a knowledge that is experienced. I am alone, completely alone, without any knowledge of Supreme Goodness, save for a strong, yes, but futile desire to love this Supreme Goodness.

In the midst of this total abandonment, I am forced to live when at every moment death is a desirable relief from this excruciating existence. Alas...my God, my God! In the profound bitterness of my heart where I find myself condemned, I am allowed to utter no other lament than, *Why have you abandoned me?* In vain were the modest efforts I made to endure such a ferocious passion. I am deprived of life; it is no longer worth bearing and resisting. It is urgent that I either live of You and in You and with You, or that I die. Either life or death! My hour is terrifying, my father, and I do not know how to drag myself beyond it. And who knows how much longer this terrible hour will be prolonged.

Tell Jesus not to be tyrannical again to the point that I come to tyrannize Him myself. He makes Himself so sought after and when one searches for Him among the elect and He does not allow Himself to be found, one is terribly tempted to search for Him among enemies. It is dreadful to combat this temptation, which seems to scatter, overthrow, and knock down everything that the half-dead soul could possibly gather to make a blade of hope germinate in order to hope against hope.

My God!... What state am I in? My father, it seems useless to call for your help when death is death and the resurrection of an already rotting corpse is required. I want to suffer, that is what I long for, but if only I might know how to suffer and to bear my undoing in peace, with abandonment to God, as a just and deserved sentence for my infidelities.

I see exactly what I am, and such knowledge makes me understand how unworthy I am of any attention, divine or human. Every day I descend into the monstrous abyss of my deformity, and this makes me understand what I deserve.

My father, stop, for goodness' sake stop lavishing your precious pearls on this filthy creature who knows neither how to use nor to value them as they deserve. Acorns and worthless garbage are fitting for this filthy creature.

My father, I am trying to find my God again. I still feel within me a thread of hope, but I am still upset, seeing and confirming how pointless my goal is and just how futile my labors. The Lord works—let what I say alone—together with Satan. I am forced to swallow my condemnation, consuming the favors, efforts, sacrifices, and benefits of God and of authority that are—and may God grant that it not be in vain to the end—for my own good…

Shut off completely from the light of day, with no glimmer of light to dispel my everlasting night, I crawl through the dust of my own nothingness; I toss about in vain, powerless in the mud of my miseries of every sort. This is a just position for one who is guilty, for a proud person plunged back into the dark and difficult deep, felled by the Omnipotent who resists him. O God! What remedy would be worth crossing this ultimate limit that never ends and cuts off every hope?

O my father, it is an imperious force that makes me forget every assurance authority has given me. My God, who severs every thread of communication, rends the seeds of good-will, and renders the spirit so blind and defenseless that it is incapable of retaining the substantial food prepared for its preservation and salvation? Not without cause am I horrified while I discover through experience the truth I assert.

It is fitting justice; Your just scorn, provoked by my infidelity, urges you to this severity. I am as worthless, in Your eyes as well as in mine, as some of Your angels, and for this I deserve all Your repugnance, rejection, and abandonment. I am struck dumb, O Lord, as I consider that Your severity is the repercussion of my faults. But, my God, might I not still hope that you will return to me? I await, O my father, your answer to this frantic question.

I find myself imprisoned in this state, without respite and with ever growing anxiety since the feast of the Apostles,[69] which has made my position excruciating past all telling. And

69. This occurred during the feast of Corpus Christi and not of the Apostles Saints Peter and Paul.

this is the way it happened: I recall that on the morning of that day, at the offertory of the holy Mass, there arose within me a life-breath. I would not know how to say, even remotely, what happened inside me in that fleeting moment. I felt totally shaken, filled with extreme terror, and I nearly died. Then a complete calm as I had never experienced before occurred.

All this terror, shaking, and calm, following one after the other, was caused not by a vision, but by something I felt touch me in the most secret and intimate part of my soul. I cannot say anything more about this event. May it please God to help you understand what happened in its reality.

During this event, I had time to offer myself entirely to the Lord for the same intention that the Holy Father recommended to the whole Church in offering prayers and sacrifices. I had barely finished doing this when I felt myself plunged into this cruel prison, and I heard the rumble of the prison door locking me inside. I felt gripped by the roughest shackles, and I suddenly felt faint. From that moment on I have felt myself in hell without respite, not even an instant.

Father, forgive me. I was mistaken in the account. What I have revealed to you did not happen on the feast of the Apostles, but on the feast of *Corpus Domini*.[70] The offering I made was for the intention the Holy Father had in commi...[71]

[FRA PIO]

---

70. In 1918, the feast of Corpus Christ fell on May 30.

71. The page ends here. The rest of the text is missing. In all probability, Padre Pio refers to the *motu proprio* of Benedetto XV, *Quartus iam annus,* of May 9, 1918, which called for a propitiatory Mass for peace on the feast of Saints Peter and Paul. Cf. *Acta Apost. Sedis* 10 (1918), 225–227.

14

"I was filled with extreme terror
at the sight of a celestial Being ..."

*On May 30, 1918, Padre Pio received the "wound of love,"
which had extraordinary effects. He did not communicate this
event immediately. From August 5 to August 7 of the same
year a mystical phenomenon takes place: the "transverberation of the heart." This is a prelude to the marvel of the
stigmata, which followed on September 20, and became a
decisive turning point in his life [500].*

San Giovanni Rotondo, August 21, 1918

∾

J.M.J.D.F.C.

My dearest Father,

May Jesus be with you always and repay you one hundred-
fold for the good that you endeavor to bring to my soul!

Here I am again with the most distressing worries for you,
and with the absolute powerlessness of a defenseless and weary
spirit that writhes amid infinite difficulties and contradictions.

My God, my father, at every moment how many needs are
crowding my spirit, which destroys itself and rots in its sorrow.
At every step I find myself more adrift in the gloom and growing
disorder of the spirit, in the dark, in the mournful loss of all

powers, and in the confusion of the senses. In vain I strive to gather them back together, but everything escapes me. I think it is a fruitless effort and I cry, because no one hears me. Consequently, the aid of the angel that guides me—and who will have to give a great account to God[72]—is wasted and ruined, and even this contributes to making my martyrdom more excruciating.

As you see, father, everything becomes a condemnation for me and my clear, actual, and observed view of myself only confirms the irrevocable sentence that God may have already passed. Where will I turn? The difficulties of my condition seem insurmountable, particularly during these days of the most difficult hell. Where will I land? I have no direction; I have lost everything, perhaps forever. I no longer know the way. I no longer have a single ray of light, no stance, not even a guideline, no life, and no more truth to understand how to nourish and refresh myself. Thus, I try to hope *contra spem* [against hope] as you suggested.[73]

I am ready for anything; I strive to dispose myself for anything, but I have neither the means nor the way to be able to arise to the daylight once again or to help myself with memories and support, since everything is devoured and destroyed[74] by some obscure force that indeed must be powerful. O Way, Truth, and Life! Give my soul what it needs before I am submerged in this vast ocean, this abyss that invites and draws me so as to inevitably devour me!

---

72. The same letter, with some variation, was sent on the same date to Father Agostino.

73. In Father Agostino's letter: *as suggested by you and by the provincial father.*

74. A., he omits: *and destroyed.*

My father, I do not have the strength to endure this excruciating martyrdom, this horrendous carnage, and this is the third day that I am forced to remain in bed powerless. It seems to me that if things continue like this for just a while longer, I will no longer call on you. When the heat suffocates my spirit and the impossibility truly becomes too great, what will I do then? The assault is strong and formidable on every side, on every surface, on all matters, touching every point, every view, every depth, and every virtue is put to the test.

My God! Is this not truly the abandonment of the Lord, of a God powerful in words and deeds? Ah yes, my father, I am discovering that it is God who does all of this. But without Him what can I do if not resign myself to being swallowed by the storm that thunders furiously around me? And in the depths of the sea will I find everlasting death? The vision is clear and it strikes and shoots through me; and if even a breath of purity existed within me, I would[75] wither and be moved to believe the contrary.

From the sweet and profound sense He left in His sudden passage, I am well aware of the absence of Sovereign Good in me. O that I might not resist the supreme severity of a wise, just, and good Lord! I would say to hell, "Take me, for it is only right, and He is just and holy, but I cannot bear to think of myself resigned to the light of that vision, which is everlasting death to my spirit, for God, Eternal Light and Wisdom."

Come,[76] father, down into the secrecy of my spirit full of so many miseries and imperfections. I cannot expose them to you,

---

75. In the manuscript, as in the letter to Father Agostino: *I would leave.*

76. A., he adds: *with me.*

but it seems to me that they are innumerable, and certainly to tell of them drives others to repugnance, just as rejection is manifested by the mouth to the God of purity.

I find no way to mitigate God's just anger if not by pleasing His heart, and I cannot find the way to do that. I see that all I receive from Him—and have obtained for Him—are thorns, and this is not merely an impression; the reality shines in all its clarity. I do my best to come out of this woeful state, but I find myself defeated—without knowing or wanting to be—by the evil I really do not want to do. Ah! Where will I find shelter from the lightening bolts of a God who thunders and strikes?...

But enough[77] of my screaming. It is better that he who has the duty to keep silent to be silent, for at this point he has reached the fullness of defeat. I despair of everything, but not of Him who is Life, Truth, and Way. Of Him I ask everything and to Him I abandon myself, since He was and is everything for me. Alas! My Good! I would have been Yours forever if I had known to surrender myself to Your seductive charms. But it is fitting that I bow down before this fatal truth, but true just the same, that is the one and only truth befitting me: perhaps I may lose You forever.

My father, do not scold me. I am beside myself and I allow myself to be carried along by what I see and feel. My fruitless attempts to adhere to my guide[78] and to obedience lead me to dismay and discouragement, though I always repress and suffocate them at their first movements.

I will not cease crying out for help, but, O God, was it not always most futile to extend a paternal hand to the one blinded

---

77. A.: *sufficient.*

78. A.: *to the guides.*

by everlasting death and blindness? That is to say, set aside your help for one who knows how to be worthy of it. Valuable as it is, I feel too greatly the weight of responsibility for it. And is it not perhaps futile, since my case is indeed a hopeless one? I am too confused by the always greater contradiction between the sinister light cast on my spirit and the gentle light of which you, my guide, tell me.

I admit the truth that I have almost no more strength to continue my struggle. I am dying of hunger before a table richly set. I am burning of thirst under a spring that rushes with pure water...What else? The light blinds me before it lifts the fog from me. How is that? I am tired of further tiring my guide,[79] and this support and obedience alone are a buttress so that I do not give in to complete abandon. In executing obedience, I am persuaded to reveal to you what happened to me from the evening of the fifth and throughout the sixth of this current month.

I do not deserve to tell you what happened during this period of supreme martyrdom... I was hearing the confessions of our boys on the evening of the fifth, when suddenly I was filled with extreme terror at the sight of a celestial Being who presented himself before the eye of my intellect. He had in his hand some kind of weapon, similar to a very long iron blade with a sharp tip that looked as if it were spewing fire.[80]

At the same moment that I saw all of this, I saw the Being violently hurling the weapon into my soul. With difficulty I let out a cry; I felt I was dying. I told the boy to leave [the confes-

---

79. A.: *my guides.*

80. A., he omits: *tip.*

sional] because I was feeling ill and I no longer had the strength to continue.[81]

This agony lasted, without interruption, until the morning of the seventh. I cannot even tell you what I suffered during this period of great anguish. I even saw my internal organs torn and ruptured by that weapon, and everything was put to the sword and fire. From that day on I have been mortally wounded. In the depths of my soul I feel a wound that is always open and that causes me to writhe continually.

Is this not some new sentence inflicted upon me by divine Justice? You be the judge of the truth contained in all of this and to say if I am not completely right to fear and be extremely anguished.

I kiss your hand with profound respect and veneration, and, asking for your holy blessing, I am ever,

your poor, humble son,

FRA PIO, CAPUCHIN[82]

---

81. A.: *because I was not feeling well and I could not continue confession any longer.*

82. A.: *Your most affectionate son, fra Pio. Beginning today, I send my most sincere and cordial wishes for your name day, which I shall repeat to Jesus with the most lively insistence.*

15

"My wound, which was reopened, is bleeding."

As with the Old Testament prophets, Padre Pio does not grasp intellectually what is happening to him. It is through a listening of the heart that he is given the gift to understand. Of particular interest in this letter is his mention of "the bleeding wound" [504].

San Giovanni Rotondo, September 5, 1918

~

J.M.J.D.F.C.

My dearest Father,

May Jesus be with you always and reward you for all you do for my soul![83]

I received your letter and, full of recognition and gratitude, I thank you for what you told me [in it]. And now I turn to you again with bleeding soul, seeking living breath once more. The agony keeps growing in intensity and leaves the thread to which my miserable existence is attached very weak. And now I tremble in fear that this weak thread will at last break and, in so doing, my existence will fall into the hands of the ruin decreed

---

83. On September 6, Padre Pio addresses the same letter to Father Agostino, inserting a few slight variations, as indicated.

[for it], which seems to be imposed without allowance for any extenuating circumstances or desistance.

My trembling and fear are not unfounded. I see and am aware that this thread is becoming very thin, and it seems that my efforts to cling to it bring me to the same end: after fruitless attempts I must endure the harshest torment of seeing myself reduced to powerlessness and I must lower my arms from weariness. It appears that the fleeting rays of light that try to give me hope in the very impossibility of these efforts become more and more scarce. Alas! O God!... I have nothing but the delirious cry of a victim who, unbeknownst to him and without his complicity, consent, or strength—which has already wasted away[84]—is under the power of conflicting adversaries in a ruthless war. Meanwhile, he is actually an object and decoy for such complete and persistent violence.

The battle is furious and, what is more, because of the extreme frailty of the soul, it places this terror among its most hidden secrets, which reduces it to the most painful fainting spells. My father! May the powerful Lord at last crush the proud, frail spirit that tries to resist and at every instant receives a rain of fire for his failure.

Father, from my earliest years I have asked that the light of grace disclose to my eyes an intimate and clear knowledge of myself as the good God knows and sees me. And now that we have reached the fullness of these visions, the two opposing portraits crush the creature who, vile and unworthy, tries again in vain to cling to everything. And having fully recognized and acknowledged what this everything is worth and, ah!, seeing again how it is such a monstrosity and aberration, its mind

---

84. A., he adds: *on account of its futile struggling.*

cannot bear to look upon itself and yet must see what is its supreme torment.

My father, I would like to empty my heart to you; I would like to tell you of the actual condition of my being and give you understanding, but this power is not given to me from above. The more I renew my efforts, the more I distance myself from what is true; neither am I given the full ray of light—which darts about and illuminates in order to humble—that withdraws and disappears just as I am about to grasp it.

I am immersed in an ocean of fire. My wound, which was reopened, is bleeding, always bleeding. This alone would be enough to kill me a thousand times over or more. O my God, why do I not die? Or do You not see that the life You have chosen for this soul is one of torment? Are You also cruel, You who remain deaf to the clamor of those who suffer and You do not comfort? What am I saying?... Forgive me, father, I am beside myself and do not know what I am saying. The excessive pain that this ever-open wound causes me infuriates me against my will. It makes me go out of my mind and leads me to delirium, which I am powerless to resist.

Tell me clearly, father: Do I offend the Lord in the excesses into which I fall? What must I do so as not to displease the Lord if the attack is sudden and I have no power to resist? My God! ... May my physical life soon end if every effort to rise from spiritual death is, in fact, to no avail. I think heaven has closed itself to me and every outburst and groan returns as an arrow to mortally wound my poor heart. My prayers seem to no avail, and even in the first attempts to regain entrance my discouraged spirit finds Him, who divests it of all courage and power, disheartening it[85] in its absolute impotence and nothingness, in its inability to venture on, though soon it risks again only finding itself reduced to the same powerlessness once more.

My God, who knows this well, send some light to my [spiritual] guide so that he might discover what I do not: the true source of Your creature's many evils. My powers have never been so inert and blocked. O what bitterness this is for the will, memory, and intellect! I think that for a will that at least wants and desires the good the pain suffered is inconceivable. How much more bitter, then—for one enriched by a vast memory of the Divine wealth in all His attributes and uprightness, and, in his own regard, the duties and respect due to his Creator—is the impenetrable harshness of the death he mysteriously reflects in the ebb and flow of the wretchedness of the misery that imprisons and holds, blinds and snatches away from that cherished store of wealth.

The intellect is ground in a press and rendered unseeing by a blindness so painful that only one who has experienced this can give certain proof of its existence. Above all then, I think[86] that for an intellect awakened by such trials and placed in contrast to the most splendid rays of true life—that wanes from the moment of birth—the pain becomes completely intolerable.

I have no more strength, yet I force myself, O father, to continue pouring out to you the entire murky tide that has

---

85. A., he adds: *and reducing it.*

86. Until the end of the paragraph, the letter to Father Agostino reads as follows: *for an intellect that has become excessively sensitive and almost pilloried by the most splendid rays of the true life that wanes in it from the moment of its birth.*

emptied into my soul so that you might reflect upon it in the divine light and be able to help me to purify everything of fault. It seems to me that all the evil tendencies of the old man are in vogue and the clamor of these evil inclinations as well as the awakened and most vivid sensitivity do not cause the slightest shock or scratch to his most intimate depths. And I have the courage to stand by to watch and to see myself ever inert[87] as always and incapable of diverting my eyes and mind, so intensely concentrated on this iniquitous scene.

What has happened? I have an ever attentive Satan beside me making his vivid suggestions.[88] I make every effort to fight him, but I see that I would be powerless to know how to free myself even with a more energetic will. Though I fear he has nothing else to gain, I see him always around me and always returning to his assault. Therefore, he has already gained something and hopes to gain more still.

My God, is it possible that my existence must be a constant displeasure to you? The attack advances, O my father, and strikes me at the center. It seems that even holy obedience, which was the last remaining voice that kept my decaying strength steadfast, now surrenders under this satanic influence.

At all costs I want to believe in this voice, and in deeds I do believe in it—never mind whether it is a belief of the lips or of every ounce of the will—though I know that this voice of obe-

---

87. The rest of the paragraph in the letter to Father Agostino is as follows: *not wishing to give my approval for death, instead, yes; but without knowing or wanting—I know not which—to force myself to divert my eyes and my mind elsewhere, which have become concentrated on this most mournful picture.*

88. Here is where the part of the letter identical to that sent to Father Agostino on September 6 ends.

dience is drowning in a fury of anxieties and torments. So, after the fleeting comfort it brings, my soul plummets into a more cruel bitterness and drinks in great gulps the bitter chalice without any comfort and unconscious of the reason for my sufferings or for whom I suffer.

My God! Reduce me to an acknowledgment of my faults and bind me to a sincere contrition and solid conversion of heart.

Father, commend me and have me commended to God until I transgress no longer.

Father, in concluding, I ask you, for the love of Jesus, to please spare me for now from having to go to you. I feel very poorly both physically and morally and I feel incapable of facing the trip. For pity's sake, please do not torment this victim even more under the aspect of good. Jesus will reward you. I promised to come and I will keep my promise, but it is impossible for me at the moment.

I kiss your hand and I ask your blessing.

FRA PIO, CAPUCHIN

∾ 16 ∾

"Holy obedience is the last voice."

In the face of the trial of evil, anxieties, torments, and perhaps even bitterness may be present, but according to Padre Pio the practice of "holy obedience"—fulfilling the will of God the Father by conforming to the example of Jesus (cf. Jn 6:38)—must never wane. It is a model that follows three criteria: fulfilling the Father's will without having one's own plans, not advancing one's own will before God's and, above all, doing the will of the Father as a "yes" to the Holy Spirit [505].

San Giovanni Rotondo, September 6, 1918

∾

I.M.I.D.F.C.

My dearest father,

May Jesus be with you always and may He reward you for all that you do for my soul!

I received your letter a while ago and, full of gratitude and appreciation, I thank you for what you said in it.[89]

What is happening? I have a vigilant Satan beside me with his vivid temptations, and ever inert, I look upon all of this

---

89. Essentially this is the same letter as that addressed to Father Benedetto on September 5.

because I am powerless to understand how to free myself of him with a will that I wish were energetic.

The attack advances, advances, and advances ever more, and it strikes me at the center. Even holy obedience, which was the last remaining voice that kept my declining strength steadfast, is now at risk. My God!… What will happen to this creature of Yours?

Assurances drown in a fury of anxieties and torments, because He who is omnipotent knows how to destroy the light and any impression of comfort simply because the soul must remain in torment; and after the drop of honey, it is forced to press its lips to the most bitter chalice and drink from it until there is nothing but the dregs.

May Your eternal and just decrees be accomplished in Your creature, O God of love, but leave me the strength to hope against hope!

Father, I end here. I have no more strength to continue.

Commend me to Jesus, and I will constantly do the same for you. I pray you to rest assured because Jesus is happy with you and your trial is nearing its end.

Please return my regards to the doctor.[90] I am pleased and I thank God for the pleasant company God has sent to you. He is truly a good son, but even good sons sometimes do some wrong to paternal goodness. He, too, gambled away grace for an excess that he committed in a moment of extreme trial.

Bless me always.

Most affectionately,

FRA PIO, CAPUCHIN

---

90. Evidently this is a reference to Dr. Luigi Romanelli.

∾ *17* ∾

"God does not come to heal old wounds,
He opens new ones."

This letter begins the third period of correspondence from San Giovanni Rotondo. Padre Pio experiences the love of God with profound clarity. In fact, the holy man knows that God "does not give time to time," when he loves. When God hides His presence, it is not through what Padre Pio refers to as the "old wounds," but through the "new" wounds God opens [508].

San Giovanni Rotondo, October 17, 1918

∾

J.M.J.D.F.C.

My dearest father,

May Jesus, the Sun of Justice, shine ever brightly in your spirit!

Here I am returning to you after a very long period of silence and you will, of course, forgive me, knowing that it was not due to negligence or indifference but absolute powerlessness. I was even bedridden with the Spanish fever,[91] which is

---

91. The Spanish Influenza pandemic of 1918–1919 is attributed with causing 20 to 40 million deaths in one year, more than the total fatalities of World War I.

wrecking deadly havoc even here. How desirable it would have been if the Lord had called me to Himself, but He gave me back to this miserable existence to struggle in time.

I have spent and spend terrible and sad hours that cause me at every turn physical and moral death. God is unfamiliar to my spirit! O love of my soul, where are You? Where are You hiding? Where can I find You? Where can I look for You? Do you not see, Jesus, how my soul longs to hear and feel You at any cost? It looks everywhere for You, but you do not allow Yourself to be found except in the fullness of Your fury, filling the soul with extreme tribulation and bitterness, making it understand how much this befits You and how much the soul belongs to You. Who can express the seriousness of my position?! What I understand in the reflection of Your light I cannot utter in human language, and when I wish to stutter something of it, my soul discovers it has erred and is even further from the truth.

My Good! Am I deprived of You forever? I have the desire to cry out and lament with an extremely strong voice, but I am very weak and no strength attends me. In the meantime, what can I possibly do but have this lament ascend to Your throne: *My God, my God, why have You abandoned me?*

My entire soul is poured out over the clear scene of my misery! My God! May I bear such a mournful sight; withdraw from me the reflection of your light for I cannot endure such an apparent contradiction. My father, I see all my wickedness and ingratitude in complete clarity; I see the old broken man turned in on himself, wanting to retaliate against God for His absence, denying God His due, that is his strictest duty. And what force is needed to raise him up! My God! Come to my aid quickly, for I tremble for myself, a wicked creature, ungrateful to his Creator, who would protect him from his powerful enemies.

I did not know how to avail myself of Your favors, O Most High, and now I see myself condemned to live in my inability, turned in on myself in the act of going astray, and the weight of Your hand grows heavier over me. Alas! Who will free me from myself? Who will pull me out of this body of death? Who will extend a hand so that I am not enveloped and swallowed in this vast, deep ocean? Is it necessary that I resign myself to being wrapped by the tempest that always presses onward? Is it necessary that I pronounce a *fiat* when I see that mysterious Being, who wounds me all over and does not desist in its harsh, rough, sharp, and penetrating action, and does not give time for the healing of the old wounds, but opens new wounds on top of them, causing the poor victim infinite torment?

Alas! My father, come to my aid, for pity's sake! My entire interior being rains blood and, more often than not, I am forced to resign myself to seeing it flow even on the outside. Alas! May this torture, this condemnation, this humiliation, this confusion cease! My soul cannot bear not knowing how to resist.

There are so many things I would like to say to you still, my father, but a flood of pain suffocates me and it makes me dumb. Show me the kindness of your quick reply and be assured that I will thank you and that I will always pray for you.

Bless me always.

FRA PIO, CAPUCHIN

"I notice something like an iron blade…"

For the third time, Padre Pio sees an apparition of the mysterious Being that presented itself for the first time on August 5, the eve of the liturgical feast of the Transfiguration of the Lord Jesus. And he feels a blade… [515].

San Giovanni Rotondo, December 20, 1918

᭙

J.M.J.D.F.C.

My dearest father,

May the Baby of Bethlehem always permeate your heart, filling it with all heavenly gifts!

Here I am, back once again with my soul overflowing with sorrowful bitterness. A consuming fire engulfs me entirely and holds me in a painful faint. The thick shadows envelop me completely; a most powerful force of being, almost invisible, consumes me and, while I try again to gather the dispersed remnant of my faculties, everything goes astray again and seems crushed and annihilated.

My God! I stand before You, who are what You are, in profound confusion. I…a wretched nothing, worthy only of Your contempt and pity; but…I reflect that I am dealing with God, who is mine. Ah, yes! And who would deny Him to me?

My father, in rereading your repeated assurances and exhortations,[92] I wonder at the impossibility of penetrating myself interiorly as I would like; I wonder if, in my believing without hearing, there might be something harmful to the spirit, if there might be some lack of conformity willed by God.

Alas! The feelings that rise up in me in this regard touch two extremes, colliding with each other and reducing the soul to a near powerlessness to react, holding it in this most cruel martyrdom day and night.

Aias! Where am I? What is happening to me? Where can I possibly find God?[93] Where is my God? My search is an illuminated circle that always brings me back as much to the beginning as to the end. I do not understand your suggestion to leave this alone—even when I am not permitted to do so. Do me the charity of explaining this to me.

Father, when will the persistent torment I feel in my soul and body ever end? My God, my father, I cannot bear it any longer. I feel myself dying a thousand deaths at every instant. I feel myself devoured by a mysterious, intimate, penetrating force that always holds me in a sweet, yet most painful faint.

What is this? Is it a fault to lament to God about such harshness? And if it is a fault, how does one stifle such lamentations when a power, which one cannot resist, forces me to voice my lament to the sweet Lord without my being able to stop it in any way?

For several days now I have noticed within me something like an iron blade extending from the lower part of my heart

---

92. In Father Agostino's letter, he adds: *and the letter written to me by the provincial father.*

93. A., he omits: *Where can I…God?*

straight across to my right shoulder. It causes me the sharpest pain and does not allow me the least bit of rest. What is this?

I began to notice this new phenomenon after another apparition of the same mysterious Being—of which I have spoken, as you will recall, in my other letters—from August 5 and 6, and October 20.[94]

Tell me everything in your reply and calm me.

For the coming[95] feast of Baby Jesus, I wish your heart to be his flowery cradle in which He might lie down without discomfort and without any offense for that *Exivi a Patre et veni in mundum.*[96]

With veneration and the greatest respect I kiss your hand and, asking for your holy blessing, I remain,

Your most affectionate son,

FRA PIO, CAPUCHIN

---

94. Evidently he is referring to September 20, but both this letter to Father Benedetto and the copy addressed to Father Agostino read October 20. Actually, in Father Agostino's letter, Pio had written "September" and then substituted it with "October."

95. A.: *coming* is crossed out.

96. Jn 16:28.

"I am powerless to hold tight this divine Lover."

The measure of divine love offered to Padre Pio with the gift of the stigmata surpasses the limit of human strength and the capacity for containment. In fact, precisely because Padre Pio cannot contain it all, he fears that he will lose that love and labors to hold this divine Lover tight. Undoubtedly, this divine Lover is the person of the glorified Jesus Christ, and contact with Him—which even includes "the pleasure of intimate embraces"—causes temporary loss of consciousness [519].

San Giovanni Rotondo, January 12, 1919[97]

·❦·

My dearest father,

May Jesus continue to possess you in heaven, as you possess Him in your hands sacramentally every day!

Trembling, I present myself to you once again. But why do I tremble? I see that it is absolutely impossible to express the work of delight; infinite Love, in the immensity of His strength, has finally conquered the hardness of my soul and I am crushed and reduced to powerlessness.

---

97. The same letter was sent to Father Agostino.

He continues pouring Himself out entirely into the small vessel of this creature who suffers unspeakable martyrdom and feels incapable of bearing the weight of such immense love. Alas! Who will comfort me? How will I manage to carry the Infinite in my small heart? How will I confine Him in the narrow cell of my soul?

My soul dissolves from pain and love, from bitterness and sweetness at the same time. How can I bear such an immense[98] work of the Most High? I possess Him in myself, and this is reason for exultation, which moves me irresistibly to say with the most Blessed Virgin, *"Exultavit spiritus meus in Deo salutari meo."*[99]

I possess Him within me and I feel everything[100]: I feel the strength to say with the bride of the sacred book of Songs: *"Inveni quem diligit anima mea... Tenui eum et non dimittam."*[101] But when I see myself incapable of withstanding the weight of this infinite love,[102] to confine it entirely into the smallness of my existence, I am filled with the fear that perhaps because of my inability to contain it in the narrow little house of my heart, I will have to let it go.

This thought, which by the way is not unfounded (I know the measure of my strength, which is most limited, incapable, and I am powerless to hold tight this divine Lover forever), torments me, afflicts me, and I feel my heart breaking in my chest.

---

98. A., he adds: *and harsh.*

99. Lk 1:47: "My spirit rejoices in God my Savior...."

100. A., he omits: *and I feel everything.*

101. Song 3:4: "Scarcely had I passed them, when I found him whom my soul loves. I held him, and would not let him go...."

102. A.: *Lover.*

My father, I cannot survive this sorrow.[103] I feel destroyed because of it, I feel my life growing faint, and I do[104] not know whether I am alive or dead at these moments. I am beside myself. A mixture of sorrow and sweetness exist simultaneously and reduce my soul to a sweet and bitter faint.

The intimate embraces of pleasure, which then follow in great profusion and, I would almost say, without respite and without measure or relief, are not sufficient to extinguish the acute martyrdom of this soul that feels incapable of bearing the weight of infinite love. Precisely at such moments, which are virtually continuous,[105] the soul utters words to that divine Lover that cause me to shudder in horror when I am myself once again.

Alas, father! Tell me sincerely: Is Jesus offended by these expressions that smell of resentment toward His love? I would like neither to utter nor to hear them again, but a mysterious force compels me and there is neither time nor strength to resist. My God, what will I do to remedy this if it is an evil?

O, my father, would now not be the time to leave your son in peace? What is the use of detaining him longer when living is worse than death itself? Alas, father! Stop being so cruel.

I await your very long letter, and soon.

---

103. A.: *survive this cruel martyrdom.*

104. A., he adds: *truly.*

105. A., he adds: *what's more.*

I kiss your hand with respect and, begging your blessing, I sign

Your dear son,

FRA PIO

I had the small cloth[106] sent to you. Did you receive it?

---

106. This is in reference to a "small cloth" used to dry the blood that flowed from the stigmata.

❦ *20* ❦

"What a thorn I feel driven into my heart!"

In this letter, we read how Padre Pio no longer feels divided between offering himself as victim for his brethren in exile (because of sin) and wanting to die for the Bridegroom. He unites them in a double motivation as "the high point of the spirit" [562].

San Giovanni Rotondo, October 8, 1920

❦

I.M.I.D.F.C.

My dearest father,

May Jesus be the star that always guides our steps along the desert of the present, and may He soon permit us to dock at the port of health!

With this most sincere and cordial wish, which I constantly make to Jesus for you and for me, I reply to your letter of September 27[107]—which father guardian just delivered to me a few hours ago—in the firm hope that Jesus will accept the groans of the soul that places himself and the souls dear to him in His care.

What can I tell you about my spirit? I see myself in extreme desolation. I am alone in bearing the weight of everyone, and the

---

107. A missing letter.

thought of not being able to bring comfort of spirit to those Jesus sends to me, the thought of seeing many souls dizzily justifying their evil despite the Supreme Good, afflicts me, tortures me, torments me, wears on my mind, and tears my heart to pieces.

O God! What a thorn I feel driven into my heart! Lately, I feel two forces that appear to be extreme opposites: wanting to live in order to be of use to my brethren in exile and wanting to die so as to be united with the Bridegroom. I feel these forces magnified to the greatest degree in the height of my spirit. This rips my soul and takes away its peace, though not its innermost peace. Even if it could touch that peace, let us say, outwardly only, I still know that it is most necessary for me in order to act with greater gentleness and unction.

Ah! My father, do not leave me alone; help me with your prayers and your advice. I tell you, I feel a solitude that deprives me of calm and of rest, and even of my appetite. If things continue this way, then we are on the eve of a great crisis, since even my physical body suffers the same effects as my spirit, though I fear more for the former than the latter, not for myself, but entirely and exclusively for others.

And how are you? I hope that you enjoy if not perfect peace, at least a sweet resignation to the divine will. All the souls united with us in the spirit of Jesus and I never cease praying for you and for all your intentions.

In the hope of receiving news from you soon, I kiss your hand with twofold veneration, with the comfort of your paternal blessing.

FRA PIO

"Belief in authority is not lacking…"

The year 1920 proved as difficult for Padre Pio as the preceding year. The previous year's medical examinations of Padre Pio's strange wounds by Dr. Giorgio Festa and Professor Luigi Romanelli, chief physician at the civilian hospital in Barletta, had to be repeated. And in April 1920, the skeptical Father Agostino Gemelli, O.F.M., visited San Giovanni Rotondo, but did not personally examine the stigmata [569].

San Giovanni Rotondo, December 20, 1920

∾·

J.M.J.D.F.C.

My dearest father,

May Jesus be your escort, support, and guide always and in everything!

On the auspicious recurrence of the holy birth of Baby Jesus, may the wishes for perennial well-being and eternal spiritual happiness be welcome.

This is the synthesis of the wishes I will offer for you before the cradle of the Infant Jesus in these holy days. May it please Him to grant them all.

In the meantime, please do not cease to commend me and to have me commended to Baby Jesus, so that he might always make me follow His will, so that His divine plans may be fulfilled in me.

The tempest of which I spoke to you about directly[108] rages on ever more. Belief in authority is not wanting and my efforts to conform increase the shooting pain of those thorns that rend my heart profoundly.

My father, what woeful and dismal days are present to my mind! What a bad Christmas it will be for me this year!

I am ready for everything as long as Jesus is happy and saves the souls of my brethren, especially those He has placed in my care.

I kiss your hand with the greatest veneration, and I ask your paternal blessing.

Your poor, humble son,

FRA PIO, CAPUCHIN

---

108. He is certainly alluding to a meeting with Father Benedetto when the latter went to Barletta for the Feast of the Immaculate Conception.

❧ 22 ❧

"Lady Gentleness seems to be doing a little better."

Padre Pio, using the traditional Franciscan title "Lady" for the various virtues, confesses to Father Benedetto that of all the virtues, especially for his temperament, he desires gentleness of character the most. In order to acquire this virtue, he asks Jesus and Mary for it with faith. He also devotes himself to the task of acquiring it through the diligent exercise of meditation [609].

San Giovanni Rotondo, October 23, 1921

❧

J.M.J.D.F.C.

My ever dearest father,

May Jesus always be entirely yours, may He transform you completely with His holy grace, and may He make you ever more worthy of His divine promises!

Your letter[109] reached me only last night, and with it the salami. I hasten to respond to thank you for your paternal tenderness, which I acknowledge myself as being ever more undeserving of in the measure that your thoughtfulness increases.

---

109. A letter that we do not possess.

Listen, my father, I am indeed filled with the tender affection you show toward me. Therefore, I ask you the kindness to no longer confound me by so generously sending such things, especially when you are depriving yourself. I ask only the kindness of being ever helped by your advice and your prayers. I do not need anything else, and, if necessary, I can willingly do without.

You tell me that I have threatened to think only of myself. I do not know if or when I said this, and to whom. In any case, even if I did say this, I need to tell you, my father, that it was not said in the way you have understood. My actions prove this. I have worked, I want to work; I have prayed, I want to pray; I have kept watch, I want to keep watch; I have wept and I want to always weep for my exiled brethren.

I know and understand that this is not much, but it is what I know how to do. This is what I am able to do, and all that I am able to do.

For heaven's sake, do not judge me with such rigor. Jesus is so good, and He is not as rigorous and demanding as I see you are. Be indulgent with everyone, above all with the one who has pledged himself entirely, and without reservation, to God and to souls.

Lady Gentleness seems to be doing a little better, but I am not satisfied. But I do not wish to lose heart. Many are the promises, my father, I have made to Jesus and Mary. I desire this virtue through their help and, in exchange, besides fulfilling the other promise I made to them, I have again promised to make it the object of my diligent meditations and yet more assiduous subject of my prayers for souls.

Therefore, father, you see that I do not remain indifferent to the practice of this virtue. Help me with your prayers and with the prayers of others.

As far as the convent at San Marco is concerned,[110] do not worry. Jesus will not permit it to be abandoned. Actually, I say this not because I had a supernatural sign, but because I feel an innermost conviction that the convent will remain ours.

I've been busy and happily continue to be busy with the publication of your book.[111] Let me know to whom I should hand over the offerings that have been given for this work.

I kiss your hand with respect and ask the charity of your prayers and the comfort of your paternal blessing.

FRA PIO, CAPUCHIN

---

110. The monastery at San Marco la Catola had been rented to the Capuchins by the local civil government until September 8, 1922. Before the lease expired on January 28, 1920, the city council informed the Capuchins that the lease would not be renewed and asked that they vacate the property immediately. The provincial superior responded by saying that the Friars could not fulfill the request, especially because of the difficultly in finding another location suited for their mission. No action was taken and the monastery remained in the hands of the Capuchins.

111. Conferences for young people.

23

"In Him I always feel rested."

The descriptive narrative of the stigmata in Padre Pio's correspondence ends with this letter. In this last fragment, the holy stigmatic details the outline of his entire spiritual life, achieved through a mystical program: to be "devoured by the love of God and by the love of one's neighbor." With the image of God permanently imprinted on Padre Pio's mind and heart, he admires "His beauty, His smiles" [611].

San Giovanni Rotono, November 20, 1921

·❧·

J.M.J.D.F.C.

My dearest father,

May Jesus always be yours, may he always assist you with his vigilant grace, and may he make you holy!

Is it possible, father, that you are never happy with yourself? Jesus holds you most dear despite every one of your demerits; He makes the graces stream down upon you, and you complain. It is about time you stopped this and began to convince yourself that you are greatly indebted to our Lord. So, less complaints, more gratitude, and much thanksgiving.

You must ask one thing only of our Lord: to love Him. And all the rest is thanking Him.

Now, for me, I first of all confess that it is a great misfortune not to know how to express and expose this whole, ever-active volcano that burns within me and that Jesus has poured into this very small heart.

It is all summed up in this: I am devoured by the love of God and by the love of my neighbor. For me God is ever fixed in my mind and imprinted on my heart. I never lose sight of Him. I have to admire His beauty, His smiles, and His agitation, His mercy, His retribution or, rather, the rigor of His justice.

With the loss of all the soul's freedom, with the binding of all its spiritual and corporal powers, just imagine by what sentiments my poor soul is devoured.

Believe me, too, father, that the outbursts of anger that I have sometimes experienced were caused precisely by this harsh and we could even say fortunate prison.

How is it possible to see God saddened by evil and not be equally saddened? To see God on the verge of letting loose his thunderbolts and, by the same token, having no other recourse than to raise one's hand to hold back His arm, while turning one's other hand to urge on your own brethren for two reasons: that they discard evil and quickly move away from where they stand, because the Judge's hand is about to let itself loose upon them?

Do believe, however, that at this moment my inner self [112] is not in any way shaken or upset in the least. I feel only to have and to want what God wants. And in Him I always feel rested, at least interiorly; on the outside I am sometimes a bit uncomfortable.

---

112. In the manuscript: *does not leave.*

And as regards the brothers? Alas! How many times—not to mention always—must I pray with Moses to God the Judge: either save this people or blot me out of the book of life.[113]

How awful it is to live by the heart! At every moment you must die a death that does not let you die except by living death and by dying to live.

Alas! Who will free me from this devouring fire?

My father, pray that a deluge of water might come to cool me a little from these devouring flames that ceaselessly burn in my heart.

Bless me always and commend me to the Divine Mercy, as in every moment I do for you.

Your most obedient son,

FRA PIO, CAPUCHIN

---

113. See Exodus 32:31–32.

BOOKS & MEDIA

The Daughters of St. Paul operate book and media centers at the following addresses. Visit, call or write the one nearest you today, or visit us at: www.pauline.org

CALIFORNIA

3908 Sepulveda Blvd, Culver City, CA 90230	310-397-8676
5945 Balboa Avenue, San Diego, CA 92111	858-565-9181
46 Geary Street, San Francisco, CA 94108	415-781-5180

FLORIDA

| 145 S.W. 107th Avenue, Miami, FL 33174 | 305-559-6715 |

HAWAII

| 1143 Bishop Street, Honolulu, HI 96813 | 808-521-2731 |
| Neighbor Islands call: 866-521-2731 | |

ILLINOIS

| 172 North Michigan Avenue, Chicago, IL 60601 | 312-346-4228 |

LOUISIANA

| 4403 Veterans Memorial Blvd, Metairie, LA 70006 | 504-887-7631 |

MASSACHUSETTS

| 885 Providence Hwy, Dedham, MA 02026 | 781-326-5385 |

MISSOURI

| 9804 Watson Road, St. Louis, MO 63126 | 314-965-3512 |

NEW JERSEY

| 561 U.S. Route 1, Wick Plaza, Edison, NJ 08817 | 732-572-1200 |

NEW YORK

| 150 East 52nd Street, New York, NY 10022 | 212-754-1110 |
| 78 Fort Place, Staten Island, NY 10301 | 718-447-5071 |

PENNSYLVANIA

| 9171-A Roosevelt Blvd, Philadelphia, PA 19114 | 215-676-9494 |

SOUTH CAROLINA

| 243 King Street, Charleston, SC 29401 | 843-577-0175 |

TENNESSEE

| 4811 Poplar Avenue, Memphis, TN 38117 | 901-761-2987 |

TEXAS

| 114 Main Plaza, San Antonio, TX 78205 | 210-224-8101 |

VIRGINIA

| 1025 King Street, Alexandria, VA 22314 | 703-549-3806 |

CANADA

| 3022 Dufferin Street, Toronto, Ontario, Canada M6B 3T5 | 416-781-9131 |
| 1155 Yonge Street, Toronto, Ontario, Canada M4T 1W2 | 416-934-3440 |

¡También somos su fuente para libros, videos y música en español!